She Gave Me Caramel Apples

A Story of Adoption and the Amazing,
Unexpected Reunion between a Mother and
Daughter

WISE
INK

ISBN 13: 978-1-63489-571-2

Library of Congress Catalog Number has been applied for.

Printed in the United States of America

First Printing: 2022

26 25 24 23 22   5 4 3 2 1

Cover design by Jack Walgamuth

Interior design by Patrick Maloney

WISE INK

Wise Ink Creative Publishing
807 Broadway St. NE
Suite 46
Minneapolis, MN 55413

This book is dedicated:

To my parents, Jack and Marion Moore Steckelberg,

To my biological mother, Phyllis Cunningham Brookbank,

And to the families of both.

What greater aspiration and challenge

Are there for a mother

Than the hope of raising

A great son or daughter?

—Rose Kennedy

This story is about 97 percent factual. The other 3 percent is me being creative and filling in some minor details, based on my knowledge of the people in the story and on my conversations with Phyllis. Some of the dialogue is imagined or re-created. In these situations, the people who had the answers are now deceased. Because of that, there are some fictitious elements to help the continuity of the story and to keep it entertaining. The story as a whole is 100 percent accurate.

Some names have been changed as:

1. I don't know the family—that is, my biological father's family—or

2. I did not get permission to use their name.

Some of the names I'm substituting are Mr. Smith and, of course, Ed.

Introduction

This story starts with Phyllis Cunningham, the youngest daughter of a midwestern middle class couple. She began her journey through life in Mitchell, South Dakota. The first part of the book is her story. It covers several chapters and is told in chronological order. Join me on this journey through her childhood and young adulthood, including her love of the Corn Palace in Mitchell and all that Mitchell has to offer, growing up during the Great Depression, life during World War II, and on to her pregnancy in 1954. At the beginning of her pregnancy, she felt joy and happiness, then as the time passed, she felt anger and disgust, and finally sadness and total upset. The world was a much different place in the 1950s for an unmarried pregnant woman. This book tells of her resilience and tenacity during those hard times.

Her story pauses at the moment she went into labor. Then begins the story of Jack and Marion Steckelberg, who were thinking of adopting. They had many discussions about adoption and being discouraged and disappointed at not having any babies. They talked often about whether or not they would choose the route of adoption, which they eventually did.

Phyllis's journey continues with her in the delivery room,

the things she was thinking about, and her feelings about her situation.

After the delivery of her baby, the story about Jack and Marion becoming parents for the first time continues. Their feelings started out as worry, fear, and unease. As the days passed, their feelings turned to apprehension, then joy and happiness.

The exact opposite of Phyllis.

The story of my journey begins with details about the important things that brought me to the same town and to the same church as Phyllis. I talk about some things that were parallel in my life and in Phyllis's life, one of those being that I was pregnant at a young age.

Phyllis and I had many parallels throughout our lives. We both loved music, both had blonde hair and hazel eyes, both had the Catholic faith in common, both were pregnant and unwed, and both had the opportunity to stay at a home for unwed mothers, just to name a few.

We had our separate lives, but we matched in numerous areas that a normal person would call coincidences. The thing is, there are so many of them that I don't believe that *any* of them are coincidental.

This story means a lot to me because, during my life, when something unpleasant happened, I trusted God to show me the reason for it in my future. I put my trust in God, and He will, in turn, show me the way.

We all recognize that there is a higher power guiding us. Some are different than others, but there is a higher power within us all. For me, that higher power is God. Things do happen for a reason. We may not know the reason right away, but it will be shown to us in the future—maybe even after death.

Not all things that happen are pleasant, of course. It can't be rosy and sunshiny all of the time. The unpleasant things that happen are, well, unpleasant, but they help us to grow as people. We all make mistakes, but we learn from them. We don't have to feel guilty about going down the wrong path. We do that sometimes, but we have to realize it and then turn ourselves around.

Our story is God given. God had His hands on mother and child, guiding and directing us every step of the way. The adoption papers were sealed, never to be opened, the baby's name known only to the mother. This is the story of Phyllis, the biological mother, and of me, Sue, her baby girl placed for adoption. Following is a glimpse of our journey through life to our joyful discovery of each other—Birth Mother and Daughter.

Phyllis sat back in her chair, looked up at the ceiling,and said, "Lord be with me."

"I have something I need to tell you. I've been holding this in for a year and a half. Please don't interrupt me, I have to get this out."

Phyllis

The best way to start this incredible story is at the beginning, the beginning being the birth of this tiny new life named Phyllis Darlene Cunningham. She was welcomed to the world on Monday, December 21, 1931.

My birth mother began her journey in life in Mitchell, South Dakota, the daughter of Thomas and Ethel Cunningham, entering the world at 10:20 a.m. and weighing six and a half pounds. She was born at home in a white two-story, three-bedroom rented house on the corner of Third Street and Mentzer Avenue. The house had large front and back yards and a huge picture window that faced paved Third Street; Mentzer was gravel.

This house was home to Thomas and Ethel and their five children, of which Phyllis was the youngest. She joined three brothers and one sister, the oldest brother almost twenty years her senior.

The Cunninghams were excited to welcome Phyllis to the family. They were a close-knit family with strong ties, and they accepted Phyllis immediately, though there were nine years difference between her and the next child. But they couldn't imagine it any other way. A new baby in the house—a new life! She was pretty too—lots of blonde hair

11

1931 Happenings

- Gallon of gas: 10 cents
- Pound of hamburger: 11 cents
- Average new home price: $6,790
- Average yearly wages: $1,850
- Average new car price: $640
- United States population: 122 million
- President: Herbert Hoover
- Thomas Edison passes away.
- The electric razor is invented.
- Nylon is invented.
- Toll House cookies are invented.
- The aerosol can is invented.
- The Empire State Building is completed.
- Battleship the game is introduced.
- Gangster Al Capone is sentenced for tax fraud and sent to Alcatraz prison.
- Las Vegas legalizes gambling.
- "The Star Spangled Banner" is officially named our national anthem.
- Most popular song: "Goodnight Sweetheart"
- The movie Frankenstein is released.
- The movie Dracula is released, starring Bela Lugosi.
- CBS goes on air.
- *Little Orphan Annie* airs nationwide on NBC radio.
- Ford ends production of Model A and prepares for the new Ford V8.

and beautiful hazel eyes—and a good baby at that. She didn't fuss a lot, and with all the people in the household, she liked to watch everyone as she lay in her cradle. One of her brothers made funny faces that made her burst into giggles. Little Phyllis got lots of attention, especially from her sister Dorothy, who was fifteen years old and excited about this new little baby girl. Dorothy was a youthful, pretty sophomore in high school with lots of friends who kept her busy, when she wasn't helping her mother at home. She was especially excited that the baby turned out to be a girl as she thought there were enough boys in the family already. Dorothy liked to carry Phyllis around the house, dancing with her and singing to her. Dorothy fed her and changed her cloth diapers. She liked to dress Phyllis in her old dresses, some of which had to be rescued from the fabric pile. Thankfully, they hadn't been cut into rags just yet. Dorothy would be Phyllis's biggest supporter throughout her life. Yes, she loved her little blonde-haired, hazel-eyed sister.

Decades later, there would be another blonde-haired girl with hazel eyes born in the Cunningham family, but with quite a different reception.

Mitchell, Phyllis's hometown, was the sixth largest city in South Dakota. It is located along present-day Interstate 90 in the eastern part of the state. Phyllis loved living there, with its small-town feel. It had everything she wanted—shopping, movies, roller-skating, parks, friends, and relatives. She had no desire to ever leave. It was just the right size town for her.

Mitchell is home to the World's Only Corn Palace. During the mid-1800s, many people were settling in South Dakota and the Midwest because of the rich soil. A few South Dakota towns built crop "palaces" during this time to entice people to settle in their town, and Mitchell was one of them. Mitchell's Corn Palace was grand, with domes and turrets on the roof and murals all around the outer perimeter. It truly looked like a palace. The murals were made with wheat, rye, sour dock (belonging to the buckwheat family), and twelve different shades of corn, all grown by local farmers. A theme was chosen each year, and the murals were designed by Dakota Wesleyan University design students. Workers attached the corn and wheat with nails or staples on a giant paint-by-number grid. The Corn Palace was a source of pride for Mitchell and the Cunningham family.

The murals were begun in late August and completed in October, just in time for the Corn Palace Festival to celebrate the harvest. Main Street was closed to cars during this time, and the street filled with games, rides, and food carts. The stores along the street had tables full of wonderful things, including caramel apples and homemade treats for sale. Tickets could be purchased to attend concerts with big name entertainers as part of the Corn Palace Festival. With all the corn, wheat, and rye on the outside, the Corn Palace served as a giant bird feeder. Inside was a gymnasium used for basketball tournaments, concerts, graduations, and proms during other times of the year.

Phyllis's high school graduation would be held there many years later, and she was looking forward to that. Until then, she would have fun riding the rides and eating the great food on Main Street Mitchell every year during Corn Palace Week.

Born in 1931, Phyllis was a child of the Great Depression. The Great Depression was a tough time for America as banks closed, people lost their savings, and jobs were scarce. It lasted almost the entire decade. The Cunninghams would gather around the radio daily to listen to their president talk about the state of the union. It was usually bleak, and Phyllis's parents were worried about the instability of the country and of their uncertain future. They were worried, but they put on a brave face for their children as they were determined to give them a good life.

Every day they sat down at the dinner table and thanked God for their meal, even if it was just a potato and some carrots. Phyllis wore hand-me-down clothes, but she didn't mind that at all, nor did she know any different. She wore dresses with ankle socks, most of which had belonged to her sister. A favorite was a pink flowery dress with a full skirt that was faded from all the wear. This dress was perfect for her active life as she liked to run, climb, and jump. She may have had a little "tomboy" in her. She was an easygoing child and a free spirit. She didn't give her parents any trouble and was generally a good kid.

During Phyllis's early years, two of her older brothers,

Clarence and Harvey, married and left home, leaving Dorothy, Gifford, and Phyllis behind. Phyllis was baptized in the Presbyterian church, and she was in tow every Sunday morning for church services. She learned to walk before her first birthday, and she played outside with the neighbor kids during her early childhood. Her birthdays were spent at home with family all around.

On one nice spring day, when Phyllis was about six years old, she and her mom, Ethel, were downtown walking. They came up to a clothing store with some dresses in the window and stopped to look at the colorful designs. Phyllis said, "Oh, what pretty dresses! Can I get a new dress today?"

Ethel replied, "Not today; new clothes aren't in the budget this year." They kept walking and arrived at their car. Ethel continued, "Your sister took good care of her clothes so they will have to do for now. I'm so sorry, honey. I'd love to get that new dress for you, but I just can't right now. When we're better able to, you and I will go shopping and you can get a new dress then." Phyllis was too young to understand budgets and money anyway, so she believed what Ethel told her. It was a time when folks had to take good care of their clothes, furniture, and other belongings so they would last a long time.

Phyllis wasn't too upset by that, but boy, she sure would have loved that new dress! But if there was anything this girl learned during this decade, it was strength and resilience. She made do with what she had and made the best of the situation. The furniture didn't match nor did the towels, and she was happy with that. Besides, it wasn't the things in life that created joy for her, it was the people around her. Phyllis felt the love of her family with every step she took, which gave her the strength she would need to get through not only the Depression but her whole life.

But oh, that dress! Phyllis needed to tell Dorothy about that dress. The two sisters were very close despite the age difference of fifteen years. "Dorothy!" exclaimed Phyllis. "I saw the prettiest dress in the window of the dress store today! I can't have it though. Mom says that clothes aren't in the budget this year."

"Yeah, it's because of this awful Great Depression," said Dorothy. She was sitting on her bed with her back against the wall, Phyllis sitting next to her. "Our dad is lucky to have a job. If it makes you feel any better, I don't get any new stuff either. I'll be glad when it's over."

"Me too!" said Phyllis. "I don't know what I'd do if I didn't have you around."

"I don't either!" said Dorothy. She jumped off the bed and went to her closet. She pulled the chain connected to the light. "Let's look in here and see if you can fit into any of my clothes. If they fit, you can have them. It'll be something different, at least. It'll be like new, kind of."

Phyllis's toys had also been Dorothy's at one time. A favorite that Dorothy passed down to her was her two-story tin dollhouse. Phyllis decorated it with rugs and curtains that she made with fabric scraps from her mom's material scrap box. She made dresses for her dolls that she designed herself. Furniture was made with pieces of wood she found in the vacant lot on the next block. A family lived in that dollhouse, the youngest a young girl, mirroring her own family.

Phyllis also loved paper dolls and designed outfits for them, getting her ideas from the dresses in the store windows. Between the dollhouse and her paper dolls, she was never bored. Playing with them, she felt loved and safe.

As the years passed, the two girls stayed close, even after Dorothy married and moved out of the family home and into her own home in Mitchell. Phyllis was just eight years old when Dorothy's first child was born just nine and a half months after her wedding. Phyllis was a constant visitor, riding her bike from her house to Dorothy's. She still looked through her sister's closet, borrowing clothes from time to time. She always returned them clean and pressed.

The two girls talked about anything and everything, from school to boys to friends to life, and more. Phyllis asked lots of questions, which Dorothy usually had answers for. She was the older and wiser one, and Phyllis trusted her judgment and advice.

The Cunninghams were some of the lucky ones to make it through the Great Depression, and they felt blessed and jubilant that they made it through in one piece. Phyllis always remembered that, though the times were hard, Ethel created a happy home for her family. Phyllis exited the Great Depression era with courage, determination, a lot of spunk, and a healthy dose of self-esteem, plus her mother made good on her promise to buy her a brand-new dress. Phyllis always looked on the sunny side of things, and what she remembered about this decade was her happy and safe home life.

She looked on life that way through the years, and, in the future, there would be another Cunningham child who would tend to look on life the same way.

Phyllis and her parents moved to a smaller house just a block away. This house came with an upright piano that Phyllis taught herself to play. It was a little out of tune, and two of the keys made a clunk sound. She ignored that and learned with the help of some books she found in the piano bench. She learned to make do.

2

Phyllis

The Great Depression was winding down, and people were getting back to work. Americans were reeling after the Depression years, but across the ocean in Germany, something else was brewing. In this trying decade, Americans went from the Great Depression years directly into World War II.

Two weeks before Phyllis's tenth birthday, on December 7, 1941, Japanese military forces launched a sneak attack on the US Pacific Fleet's base at Pearl Harbor in Hawaii, and the United States entered the war.

President Franklin Delano Roosevelt addressed a joint session of Congress the following day: "Yesterday, December 7, 1941—a date that will live in infamy—the United States of America was suddenly and deliberately attacked by naval and air forces of the Empire of Japan." Americans were listening to the president on their radios.

One of those households listening was, again, the Cunningham family. Nobody made a sound; they were wrapped up in and captivated by his every word. At the end of the broadcast, Ethel turned the knob to the "off" position on the radio. She quietly rose and walked slowly to the kitchen to start dinner, tears rolling down her face.

At the dinner table that night, Clarence, Harvey, Dorothy, Gifford, and Phyllis gathered around the table. They prayed, "Lord, please protect our country, wrap your loving arms around us, and keep us safe from harm. Please protect those who are fighting at Pearl Harbor and those who are enlisting. We thank you, Lord. Amen."

Ethel and Thomas wanted to know who of their sons would be going to war. "Is anyone at this table joining the armed forces?" asked Ethel. She continued, "Harvey, I know you were talking about going into the Army. Have you gotten the call yet?"

Harvey replied "Yes, I did. I've officially joined the Army and will be going to basic training somewhere in Texas, but I don't know if I'll have to go overseas or not. I have to leave next week." A collective gasp could be heard from everyone at the table.

"Next week already? Oh dear," said Ethel, on the verge of tears. "Your poor wife. And you'll miss the birth of your first baby."

"Yes, but I have no choice in the matter," replied Harvey.

"Clarence, have you heard anything? Will you have to go too?" asked Thomas.

Clarence replied, "I didn't get orders, so I will stay back at the home front and help wherever I can." Ethel brought out the dishes of food that she was serving for supper.

"Well, that's good news," said Thomas. He spooned some

mashed potatoes onto his plate and passed them down. "Gifford, I know you were talking about the Coast Guard. What are your plans?"

Gifford said, "I'll be joining the Coast Guard very soon and will be heading for Alaska. I don't have my orders yet."

Dorothy felt a lump in her throat and said, "Harvey and Giff, with our country under attack, I understand why you feel the need to join the military." Dorothy had tears in her eyes. "I wish you didn't have to go, but I really do understand. And Clarence, some of us have to stay behind to keep things going here on the home front. I'm proud of all of you."

After Harvey and Gifford left for their duty stations, Ethel hung a Blue Star Service Banner with two blue stars in the window. Each star signified a son from that household who was in the service.

It didn't seem fair to go from the Great Depression, when it was so hard to make a living or even to eat, to the World War II years, when a lot of things were rationed, such as sugar, gas, butter, milk, meat, coffee, and jellies. A lot of these items were needed for our troops and the war effort, which caused a shortage in America. These items and others had to be purchased with stamps, and only a small amount of each was allowed. The Cunningham household now found itself using those stamps. Things had been looking up, and now this. But life had to go on as usual. Thomas and Ethel kept their household running, although were creative when it came to meals—again. They needed to make their home life as normal as possible—again—

even with their two sons serving their country and possibly going overseas at any time.

Ethel noticed that some of the blue stars on the banners had changed to gold stars around town, meaning the son from that house had been killed in action. Ethel prayed for those families, as well as for her own family, especially for Harvey and Gifford.

3

Phyllis

Life continued on in America while our boys were fight-ing overseas in World War II. Phyllis's grade school years flowed into her junior high years in the mid-1940s. World War II was winding down, and Harvey and Gifford served their country stateside—Harvey in Texas and Gifford in Alaska. The Cunningham family was very relieved that the war was over and the family remained intact.

High school was much more fun for Phyllis. She learned to drive at fifteen. She was turning boys' heads with her beauty and gorgeous figure. She was getting boy crazy, which made her parents nervous, and she loved roller-skating so much that she went to the skating rink every weekend. Some of those weekends were spent with Clarence's daugh-ter Delores, who was four years younger than Phyllis, but they hung around together and were very close. Between roller-skating, shopping with her friends, meeting boys, and attending dances, she was having the time of her life.

Ethel said, "Phyllis, don't get in a hurry to get a boyfriend. You're only fifteen and too young to be dating."

Harvey		Dorothy	Phyllis	Clarence
	Thomas	Gifford	Ethel	

Phyllis replied, "I know, Mom, I won't date until you say it's okay to do so."

There were the occasional times when Phyllis would cry on her mom's shoulders because a boy she liked didn't ask her to the school dance or she was disappointed in a boy who had acted foolishly, which did happen once. A boy in her class asked her to the school dance one year, but when he was around his friends, he was acting like an idiot and being disrespectful to everyone. She had enough of that and walked home. When she got home, Ethel said, "Home so early, Phyllis?"

"Yes," she said, fuming, "That guy was an idiot, and I don't ever want to see him again." To a teenage girl, these events are monumental and earth-shattering, but she made it through those crazy teenage years just fine.

Thomas and Ethel decided that Phyllis was responsible enough to date in her junior year. She went on a couple of dates, but the boys weren't really her type. She enjoyed her last two years of high school and was looking forward to going to college. She had been working at a clothing store part time to save money for college, and she made it through her high school years in one piece.

Phyllis graduated from Mitchell Senior High School in 1949, the graduation ceremony taking place at the Corn Palace. She decided to take some business classes at Dakota Wesleyan University starting in the fall. Until then, she was going to enjoy her summer off.

She started her classes in the fall. After what her parents had to sacrifice during the Great Depression years and then the war years, she was not going to accept money from her dad.

"Phyllis," said Thomas, "Your mom and I want to pay for your college courses at Dakota Wesleyan University."

Phyllis replied, "Dad, I appreciate that very much, but you and Mom sacrificed so much for me these last few years that I think I can manage it all right. I saved the money from my job from last year, and I think I can go to school and work part time."

Thomas replied, "Okay, but if you need some help, let us know."

College, it turned out, was more expensive than she thought, but she did not want to take money from her parents. If she couldn't pay for it herself, she would quit. She went one semester and then quit.

There was only one thing left to do, and that was to get a full-time job. Phyllis was hired as the bookkeeper at a concrete company in Mitchell after her short time at college, earning paychecks and (oh boy) money to spend. She liked her job a lot and liked the owners and the other employees. She worked eight to five, Monday through Friday, with an hour for lunch each day. After working there for several months, she saved up enough money to buy her dream car—a 1949 Plymouth. It was light green with yellow seat covers that she had professionally reupholstered in fabric and vinyl. She loved showing off that car and drove all around Mitchell on her time off. Her car was one of a kind and well known in town. It was so pretty and so fine that people would stop and watch her drive by.

Phyllis received a promotion to head bookkeeper in 1952, so she decided it was time for her to get her own apartment. It was nice living with her parents, but she was ready to have her own place. She rented a small one-bedroom apartment on one of Mitchell's main streets. She furnished it with extra furniture acquired from various family members. Nothing matched, and she was all right with that. She had an eclectic taste in decorating, but she did like brightly colored pictures on the walls. She loved her newfound freedom and independence. She missed her parents, but only a tiny bit. The road ahead seemed bright, and she couldn't wait to see what was coming next.

4

Phyllis

PHYLLIS AND ED

Phyllis and Ed met on a weekend in the summer of 1953. Ed was seventeen, fresh out of high school, and worked full time on the family farm outside of Mitchell. Phyllis was twenty-one, had been out of high school for four years, and held a full-time job in town, plus she had her own apartment. Both had nice cars and liked to show them off by driving up Main Street, turning around in a parking lot, and driving back down again. They called it "dragging Main," and this activity was very popular with the young people. Main Street was lined for several blocks with stores of all kinds, including a theater and a shoe repair shop. Loud music could be heard up and down Main, with the sounds of Buddy Holly blasting from the car radios. It was a good way to meet people and to find parties on the weekends.

One warm Friday evening, Ed and his friends were dragging Main and spotted a car full of girls they wanted to meet and talk to. They had seen that car around town before, and they wanted to see it up close. The pretty girls who came with the car were a bonus. Upon passing them once more, Ed's friend leaned out the window and yelled, "Meet us at the parking lot at the end of Main!" At the appointed meeting place, everyone got out of their cars. Phyllis's and Ed's eyes met, and the attraction was instant.

Ed had seen Phyllis before and noticed her gorgeous Plymouth car right away. But when he caught a glimpse of her, he just had to meet her. She was beautiful: blonde with hazel eyes, curves in all the right places—she was a knockout. Ed was tall, dark, and handsome—dark from working in the sun on the farm and muscular to boot. And was he ever cute.

"Hi!" said Ed, looking over her car. "I've been seeing you driving around town and wanted to meet you and see your car up close. She's a beaut!" He walked around the car, looking at the hood, the tires, and the doors. He opened one of the doors to see the upholstery. "Wow, what a great car!" he exclaimed.

"Thanks!" replied Phyllis. "This is my dream car! I've seen you around too. Are you from Mitchell?" She couldn't believe she was standing there talking to this guy. He was *so* rugged, handsome, and athletic.

"I live on a farm outside of town. I help my dad with the farm work, but I get out on the weekends. Hey, we were just heading to the drive-in for a cherry Coke. Do you want to join us there?"

"Sounds great!" said Phyllis. "We'll meet you over there."

They drove up to two empty spots, and soon, a waitress on roller skates came out to take their orders. Ed and Phyllis stood at the back of Ed's car for an hour or two, talking, drinking cherry Coke, and having a wonderful time.

"What's your birth date, Phyllis?" asked Ed.

"December of 1931, how about you?" replied Phyllis.

Ed had a horrified look on his face. "Oh no, mine is February of 1936."

Now it was Phyllis's turn to be horrified. She was counting on her fingers to four years. "1936? Really? Did you just graduate from high school?"

"Yes, in May. Wait, I'm what, four years younger than you?" She nodded yes. She looked horrified.

"Wow, what do you think? Are you okay with having four years' difference?" asked Ed.

"I'm okay with it if you are," replied Phyllis.

"I am." It was time for Ed to get home, and he asked Phyllis, "Would you like to go to a movie with me next Saturday night?" He had never dated a girl who was interested in cars or who was older than him.

"Sure," replied Phyllis. "I'd love to!" She gave him her phone number and address. The movie started at seven o'clock, so they made plans for him to pick her up at six thirty.

"See you Saturday!" said Ed. He and his friends then left the drive-in.

Phyllis and Ed had a great time on their first date. They went to the movie and stopped at the drive-in for a cherry Coke afterward. Many more of those dates followed. They found that they had very much in common. Both had four siblings, both loved cars, and both were outgoing. They hit it off so well that they spent almost all of their free time together after that, going to movies, to dances, out to eat, or just for a nice drive. Now when they "dragged Main," it was in his car with Phyllis sitting right next to him. They enjoyed being together and had a great time wherever they happened to find themselves. Phyllis's friends also had boyfriends, and they went on double dates together often. Phyllis and Ed discussed their age difference but decided that four years wasn't that much, and they were okay with it. They were just hoping everyone else would be too.

When Phyllis got together with family, which was often, she invited Ed to come with her. They liked him immediately. They enjoyed his company, and he fit right in. But they were a little skeptical of the age difference. Dorothy asked Phyllis privately, "Are you sure you want to go steady with a boy just out of high school?"

Phyllis replied, "I know there is a difference in our ages, but Ed really is more mature than seventeen. Besides, four years isn't *that* much of a difference."

She and Ed could talk about anything and everything. They knew a lot of the same people. Ed spent most of his growing-up years working on the farm, tending to the hogs and sheep. He had a good sense of humor and put his mind to whatever task was at hand. One thing Ed had been wanting to do since he was a young boy was to join the Army National Guard and follow in his older brother's footsteps. Ed loved his country and felt the urge to serve, so he joined the National Guard in the spring of 1954. He was very busy with his commitment to the Army, the family farm, his friends, *and* a girlfriend. And between Phyllis's job, boyfriend, and family, she barely found time to sleep.

Yet Phyllis and Ed were able to find lots of free time to be together in the midst of all that, and they fell in love. That spring, Ed decided to introduce his family to Phyllis. By then, they had been dating for a few months, and he was ready for this next step as he felt that she was "the one" for him.

Ed was from a Catholic family, and his faith was very important to him. He and Phyllis talked about religion a lot, and he taught her some of the Catholic prayers.

One day in April, Ed took Phyllis to the farm to introduce her to his family and give her a tour of the acreage. He showed her the hogs, the sheep, the chicken coop, and the fields, then they headed back to the house. While waiting for supper in the living room, Ed introduced Phyllis to his parents. Betty, his mother, was the mother of five, a sturdy farm woman used to hard work. She arose in the wee hours of the morning and retired to bed early after a hard day of cleaning, cooking, sewing, and washing. Betty, unsmiling, said, "Hello, Phyllis."

Ed's dad got up and shook her hand and said, "Pleased to meet you."

Ed's teenage sister and brother entered the room and said hi to Phyllis. The sister had told their mother about the age difference between Ed and Phyllis. Phyllis had nephews the same age as his brother and sister, so it was easy to have a conversation with them. It was a good thing that they were there, because Phyllis was a little nervous. It didn't seem that Betty was too thrilled to meet her. To Phyllis, Betty's greeting sounded cold and insincere. She was already starting to wonder if that was because of her age. Betty called everyone to dinner at the table. Ed's family, being Catholic, said grace before every meal: "Bless us oh Lord, and these thy gifts, which we are about to receive from thy bounty, through Christ our Lord. Amen."

Phyllis already knew some of the Catholic prayers, including grace. She bowed her head properly and recited the prayer right along with Ed's family, hoping to please Betty.

Ed and Phyllis knew that Betty had some reservations about their relationship, and they had talked about it before introducing her to his family. It was true, Betty had hoped that Ed would go to college, marry someone his own age, and maybe even take over the farm someday. But he assured Phyllis that he loved her and she was his future.

"Please give her a chance," he told his mom. "Once you meet her, you'll see she is very sweet and the perfect girl for me."

Phyllis was very nervous, and she really did not feel welcome. She felt the disapproving looks from Betty from the time they arrived. She wasn't saying anything to Phyllis, she wouldn't look at her, and her greeting was not very warm or sincere. Phyllis felt uncomfortable around her already. Ed's dad seemed to welcome her, and so did Ed's sister and brother. Phyllis decided to just be herself and try her best to please Betty while at their home. She was hopeful that Betty would come around. She was probably just trying too hard, and her nervousness was getting the best of her. She chose to ignore it since this was her first time meeting Ed's family. She was optimistic that she and Betty would be friends eventually.

Time marched on, and the two of them kept busy with work and weekend activities. They visited at the Cunningham families' houses and had the occasional Sunday dinner at the farm with Ed's family. The time spent at the farm was tense for Phyllis, and it got to where she would look at the clock and wish for its hands to speed up. Betty still wasn't warming up to her, nor even looking at her. Phyllis was hoping that their two families could meet, but that wouldn't happen anytime soon, the way things were going. She hated that she felt uncomfortable and nervous around Betty, but she was determined to have a good relationship with her nonetheless. After all, she was Ed's mother, and both women loved and cared for him. Phyllis just wished that Betty would smile at her once in a while.

Betty tried to like Phyllis for Ed's sake, but she knew that Ed didn't come home until the wee hours on some mornings, and she didn't like it one bit. She was upset with the both of them. This wasn't what she had envisioned for her son. She was hoping that he would go to college and learn the financial aspect of farming, meet a girl at college, and then take over the farm. She tried to talk him into finding a girl his own age, but that wasn't going to happen anytime soon. He was eighteen and head over heels in love with Phyllis, and nothing Betty could say or do would make him change his mind.

In the meantime, Ed had saved money for an engagement ring for Phyllis. They had been together for one year now. He picked out a beautiful diamond that was small, but it sparkled brilliantly and looked perfect with the thin gold band that would go on Phyllis's finger. He didn't know the size so he had to guess, but the jeweler could size it later. Now, where and when to pop the question?

One evening in the summer of 1954, Ed took Phyllis out

for dinner, and they took a nice stroll through the park afterward. Stopping at a bench, they sat down. Ed, very nervously, kneeled in front of Phyllis and said, "Phyllis, you're the one for me. I love you. Will you marry me?" Short and sweet.

She was surprised. She wasn't expecting a marriage proposal that evening. But she didn't have to think too long about his question. He placed the ring on her left ring finger—and it fit. In that moment, the problems with Betty seemed far away. Ed wanted to marry her. She looked at the ring, then up to his face. "Yes, Ed, I will marry you," she said, smiling from ear to ear.

Newly engaged, they were very happy. They agreed they would marry in the Catholic church, and they attended mass together every Sunday. Phyllis was Presbyterian, but knowing how important the Catholic faith was to Ed, she made the decision to convert to Catholicism for him since the Catholic Church's guideline for marriage is that both have to be Catholic.

Changing to the Catholic religion is no small feat. Phyllis began Catholic education classes at Holy Family Church, meeting privately with her priest, Father Brady, every week for a few months. She learned about the Sacraments of Baptism, Communion, Confession, and Confirmation. The masses were said in Latin during the 1950s, and Father Brady gave her a book explaining what each part of the mass meant. At first, Phyllis wanted to change over to the Catholic faith to please Ed's family, but as the lessons continued, she learned to love everything that the church stood for. She liked the structure of the mass and the music. Accepting that Jesus Christ was her Savior, and that the Bible was the Word of God, she committed herself to the Catholic faith.

Phyllis was baptized in a formal ceremony at the church, and at the next Sunday morning service, called mass, she was formally welcomed into the congregation. She was a very busy girl during this period as she and Ed were also meeting with the priest for marriage instruction once a week. On one of those meetings, Father Brady asked, "Do you have a date in mind when you would like to get married?"

"What about Saturday, June 18, 1955?" replied Phyllis. "Is the church available that day?"

Flipping through the calendar, he found the month of June. "Yes, it is," replied Father Brady, making a notation on his calendar. "We'll go ahead and schedule your wedding for that day. Is there a time you have in mind?"

"How about two o'clock?" said Phyllis.

"Done," said Father Brady, as he wrote two o'clock on his calendar under June 18. Their wedding day was then officially scheduled at Holy Family Church.

Ed asked Phyllis to come to dinner at the farm one Sunday so he could announce their engagement to his family. This time, Phyllis was going to take a different approach to the situation. She knew Betty loved hymns, and she wanted to do something that would put a smile on her face. Phyllis had been practicing the song "Amazing Grace" for weeks on her piano, and she finally had it memorized. She decided to surprise Betty with that beautiful song. She was hopeful that Betty would love it. When she and Ed arrived at the farmhouse, Phyllis walked over to the piano, sat down on the bench, and lifted the lid off of the piano keys. She started playing "Amazing Grace" softly. The song sounded amazing and beautiful.

Betty could hear the music from another room, and as she was setting the table, she said, "Please stop playing my piano. Supper is ready now. It's time to come and sit down." Phyllis abruptly stopped playing "Amazing Grace" right in the middle of the song.

She was stunned. She apologized to Betty but felt hurt and angry. Phyllis was disgusted and just wanted to get this evening over with quickly. What she really felt like doing was running out the door and running the whole way home. *I don't know what else I can do. She's not going to accept me, no matter what I do*, she thought.

Phyllis had been trying so hard to get Ed's family to like her, but Betty just couldn't accept her. Phyllis was pretty sure it was all because of their ages, Phyllis being twenty-two and Ed just eighteen. Ed agreed, but he was so sure that they would love her as much as he did. Ed knew Phyllis was trying very hard to get his mother to like her. He didn't know what to do.

"Mom," said Ed, "Can't you at least try to like Phyllis for my sake? I really do love her, and I want to marry her."

Betty replied, "Ed, you just graduated from high school. You're eighteen now and an adult, but I will always be your mother, and I know what's best for you. You should be going to college and experiencing college life, maybe dating a girl your own age. Phyllis has been out of high school for four years and has a full-time job and an apartment. She's already experienced life after high school. You're just starting. There are too many years' difference in your ages."

Betty did have a point there. Ed *was* too young. She was very protective of her second-born son, and she wanted only the very best for him.

Betty continued, "Besides, there's no need to rush into marriage. What's the big hurry? Marriage is a commitment."

Ed said, "Mom, I know you mean well, but can you please be nicer to Phyllis? That's all I ask. You know I love you. You're my mom and nobody is going to replace you." Ed didn't want to say anything against his mother because he knew she had his best interests at heart. But he loved Phyllis so much, and he would do anything for those two to just get along.

After dinner, Phyllis asked Ed to take her home. Ed decided not to say anything about their engagement that evening. He felt like he was in the middle and being pulled from both sides, but he couldn't go against either one of them. It was driving him crazy. Ed really was too young to make such an important decision.

Phyllis cried on their way back to her apartment. She was so upset about spending so much time learning "Amazing Grace" on the piano only to have Betty tell her to stop playing it. "What do I have to do to get her on my side, Ed? I thought she would like it. Why can't she accept me?"

"I don't know," said Ed. "I'll talk to Mom again and ask her why she treats you like that."

Phyllis was so in love with Ed that she chose to overlook this for the time being, but she began making excuses to skip their Sunday dinners. She had come to the realization that she and Betty would never be friends. She would keep trying, but not as hard. It was a good thing Ed hadn't said anything about their engagement that day.

Phyllis's parents and siblings, however, were happy for the couple, but they knew there were problems with Ed's mother and that Phyllis was unsettled over the relationship with her. Phyllis and Ed were planning their wedding and attending church every Sunday. Phyllis was enjoying her job as head bookkeeper, and Ed kept the farm running and served his country once a month at the National Guard base. They were getting together with Phyllis's family occasionally and, less often, at Ed's. Phyllis wasn't trying so hard to make friends with Betty anymore, but she knew this was a very unusual relationship and that it was a big red flag. She knew it wouldn't be a good way to start their marriage. But she didn't know what to do about it. She chose to stay away from Betty as much as possible, and Ed was relieved that he didn't have to be in the middle of it. Deep down they both knew it wasn't right. But they stayed engaged anyway. Still no plans were made for the two families to meet.

Ed did eventually tell his parents that he and Phyllis were engaged to be married. That news went over like a lead balloon. It was like a giant boulder falling down a cliff onto the highway. *Thud!*

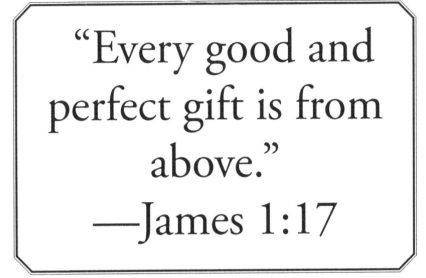

"Every good and perfect gift is from above."
—James 1:17

5

Phyllis

The 1950s were known as the baby boom generation, the postwar years. The war had ended in 1945, and America was in a state of celebration. The music was changing, and the teenagers were out to have fun. Premarital sex was getting more common, but the schools failed to educate the youth about pregnancy and prevention. Fearing that sex education would promote and encourage sexual relations, parents and schools thought it best to leave young people uninformed. Parents didn't want to acknowledge that their children could be sexually active. The only thing that forced them to acknowledge the sexual activity was pregnancy, when they couldn't avoid *that* conversation. Society failed to acknowledge the changes that were underway in the 1950s and believed that young women should wait until marriage. The only way for a girl to find out about sex was on her wedding night, or through her older friends or siblings. Sex education wasn't taught in schools until the 1970s.

Birth control was difficult to obtain as it was only offered to married women—it was even illegal in some states to sell birth control to an unmarried woman. This did not prevent premarital sex, however, and what happened was an explosion in pregnancies with babies surrendered for adoption. The girls were labeled "bad girls," but the young men who fathered those babies escaped such judgment. The girls had to drop out of school, but the boys could continue on and even stay in sports and all of the activities they were involved in.

It was the fall of 1954, and for two weeks Phyllis had been sick in the mornings. She hoped it was just indigestion but feared she might be pregnant. Her period was late. She really did not want to have to have that conversation with Ed, but she knew she was going to have to say something to him about this.

Ed came over to her apartment to pick her up to go to a movie. He made himself comfortable in her living room, and Phyllis sat down next to him. She turned to face him. "Ed," she said cautiously, "I have something I need to talk to you about." A nervous pause. "My period is overdue. I should have had it by now. It's two weeks late. I've also been feeling a little sick in the mornings. I hate to say it, but I think I'm going to have to make an appointment with my doctor and get a pregnancy test."

"Oh no," said Ed. "Is that what it means when your period is late?"

Phyllis replied, "Not always, it could just be late, but if that isn't it, what are we going to do?"

"I don't know. I don't even want to think about that. I guess it would be a good idea to get the test done at the doctor's office. We'll talk more about it after that," said Ed, dreading it already. He was worried.

Phyllis made an appointment for the next day. She dreaded this appointment and didn't get much sleep that night. She didn't tell anyone except Ed what she was doing, not even her family.

The doctor was none too pleased to have a single young woman come in for a pregnancy test, which isn't a fun one to start with. And to top it off, the doctor was a male, which made that test pretty humiliating. He said, "Please disrobe and put this sheet on, then get up on the table. I'll be back in a minute or two."

Phyllis's heart was pounding, but she did as he told her. There were some cold, hard steel things at the end of the table. She didn't know what those were for. The doctor returned. He said, "Scootch down and place your feet in the stirrups, please." Oh, so that's what those things were.

The test was horrible. His hands were in places that made her very uncomfortable. Some kind of steel instrument was inserted. It was like a nightmare. "Okay, I got a swab. I'll go check it, and I'll be right back."

The test turned out positive, and what Phyllis had feared became reality. Her doctor sat with her in that cold little exam room and proceeded to give her a lecture. Phyllis was covered in only a sheet, which made it all the more humiliating.

He scolded, "Phyllis, I've been your doctor since you were little. You have shamed your parents. They have done the best they could raising you, and this is how you repay them? I thought you knew better."

Near tears, she replied, "It was an accident. I'm engaged to be married in June of 1955, so we'll just have to move up our wedding."

The doctor pursed his lips. "Well, you'd better do that soon so the baby won't be illegitimate."

It irked her that the doctor was telling her what to do. She could make her own decisions about this situation that she was in. Her doctor was not obligated to make her decisions for her. It was up to her and Ed.

It was common in the fifties for doctors to scold the young woman and tell her to either get married or go to a home for unwed mothers and surrender the baby for adoption. The word *illegitimate* was terrible and shameful.

Shame was associated with many, if not all, of these pregnancies. Middle-class families were horrified to think that their daughter would keep an illegitimate child. It was the social stigma of being an unwed mother. These girls were often sent away to a home for unwed mothers and would "disappear" before anyone could find out why. The story was that they were visiting a sick aunt or grandmother. The girls would then return back home like nothing had happened and pick up where they left off.

Some of these girls were unfortunately given no choice but to surrender their child and were told they wouldn't have a home to come back to if they chose to keep their baby. They would have no support at all from their parents. There was no other option for those girls. And there were quite a few in that group.

There was another group of girls who were fortunate enough

to have parents willing to adopt the baby, and the baby would be raised as their own son or daughter. This was a bit awkward as the baby's mother and the baby would be raised as siblings. This scene did happen in many families.

This was the cultural moment in which Phyllis confronted her pregnancy, and although nobody had ever said it explicitly, she knew that she had to choose between marriage and adoption. At the age of twenty-two, Phyllis's world came crashing down, and the bottom dropped out of her life. She was pregnant. It wasn't a common thing for a single woman to be pregnant in the 1950s in Mitchell, South Dakota.

She wasn't looking forward to seeing Ed. After she left the doctor's office, Phyllis got in her car and sat and cried. She started the car and drove home. She waited at her apartment for Ed to get done with his chores. He came over right away, anxious to hear the answer.

Tearfully, she said, "I'm pregnant." She sat down at the kitchen table and cried.

Ed sat down on the couch and said nothing for a minute. He just sat there, staring off into space. After some thought, he said, "We need to tell our parents, and I'm not looking forward to that."

"Ed, what are we going to do?" asked Phyllis.

"We're gonna have to get married sooner," replied Ed.

"That's what my doctor said that we have to do," Phyllis responded. "But right now, I'm disgusted with him. I think we can get married whenever we darn well please. He can go soak his head in the lake."

"We don't have much time to think about that, and we're going to have to make a decision soon," said Ed.

"We should tell my parents first. I'll call Mom and see if they're free on Saturday, and I'll tell her that we have something we need to talk to her and Dad about," Phyllis said.

She then picked up the phone and called her mom. Her mom suggested that they come over for dinner on Saturday and they could sit down and talk afterward. Difficult and serious conversations were better on a full stomach. Usually.

On Saturday, Phyllis was very nervous and didn't eat much. She helped her mom clear the table after supper, then the two joined the men in the living room. Phyllis sat next to Ed on the couch. He put his arm around her. She was shaking and started crying. Thomas and Ethel were immediately concerned.

"Mom, Dad, we have something we need to discuss with you." Phyllis continued slowly, "You know I love you both very much and I never ever wanted to disappoint you. But I am in a predicament that I can't get out of, and I know you will be very disappointed in me. I need your support, now more than ever."

"Phyllis, what happened?" asked Thomas, afraid to hear her answer.

A couple of minutes passed as Phyllis began to cry. Thomas looked at Ethel. She was about to cry herself. Phyllis tried to get her courage up to say those next two words. "I'm pregnant." Ed held her tighter as she cried.

Her parents were shocked. They hadn't seen that coming.

A couple of minutes went by, then Ethel asked softly and tearfully, "Have you seen a doctor yet?"

"Yes," replied Phyllis. "I went in two days ago for the pregnancy test, and the doctor confirmed it."

Ethel sighed. "Oh Phyllis, I sure wasn't expecting that." Tears were rolling down her face.

Thomas said, "Unbelievable. I suppose you'll be getting married sooner?"

"Yes, we'll go see our priest and find out what he suggests we do," said Ed.

"To tell you the truth, I'm shocked. This was completely unexpected," said Ethel. "You're right, I *am* disappointed. I'm disappointed in you and Ed both. I thought that you would have known better. I thought we taught you to be responsible."

"I'm so sorry, it was an accident. We badly need your support," said Phyllis.

"Your dad and I are here for you for whatever you need. You always have our support no matter what. We'll talk more in a couple of days," said Ethel, as she rose from her chair and went into the kitchen. This was Ed's cue for him and Phyllis to leave.

On their way back to Phyllis's apartment, she and Ed discussed what a relief it was telling her parents. They were very supportive, which really was no big surprise. They were disappointed, yes, Phyllis knew that they would be, but she knew she could lean on them for anything and they would be there for her 100 percent.

That was a great relief and a huge load lifted off her shoulders. But she knew that they would have to break this news to Ed's parents. Oh, she dreaded that. So did Ed. She kept putting it off and putting it off for days, until Ed said, "We have to get this over with."

Phyllis knew this was not going to go well. They decided to just stop in quick, deliver the news, and leave as soon as they could.

Phyllis and Ed walked in the front door, and he called out, "Mom, Dad, are you here? Can you come into the living room?" Both appeared, puzzled. Everyone was standing. Ed said, "We have something we need to tell you, and you're not going to like it."

He looked over at Phyllis, and she said, "I'm pregnant." After a pause, she added, "Would you like to be grandparents?" There was an awkward silence.

Ed's dad just shook his head, and his mother left the room without saying a word. They were afraid that something like this was bound to happen.

Phyllis thought this announcement would be like the *Titanic* breaking apart with yelling, crying, and screaming, but it was more like scraping the iceberg; it was just a nudge. Silence. No yelling, no screaming, no crying. Ed's parents were disgusted and disappointed in them both.

Phyllis and Ed had talked about getting married sooner, but Phyllis was dragging her feet. She felt that she could wait for three or four months to see if things would improve with Ed's family. By then, she would start showing. She just wasn't too sure that she wanted to be a part of a family who didn't like her at all. It was getting to be like pulling teeth to go out to Ed's farm. Did she want this for the rest of her life? Did her baby deserve this? Would Ed's parents ever accept her baby as their grandchild? She asked herself these questions over and over again. Always, the answer was no.

Only a couple of months into her pregnancy, the arguments began. Phyllis was upset and disgusted with Ed's mother, and Ed was trying to keep the peace between the two. Arguments were increasing, Ed was working more and calling less, and they saw each other only on the weekends. Phyllis's annoyance with Betty overlapped into her relationship with Ed. These two hearts were slowly drifting apart, and she was starting to have second thoughts about marrying him. She was beginning to think that it wasn't worth the aggravation to try so hard to get Betty to like her since it wouldn't happen anyway.

She chose to stay away from the farm, as those visits were too upsetting. Ed was tired of being in the middle of it all and having to defend his parents. Phyllis and Ed were arguing more and more. She was still working at her job, which helped take her mind off things. She had people she could confide in. But with the looming breakup that was coming soon, Phyllis felt fear and extreme sadness.

She was so confused and didn't know which way to turn, so she went to see her mom to have a long heart-to-heart talk with her. She needed to get her head on straight. "Mom, I don't know what to do. I love Ed, but his mother won't even talk to me, and when she does, she's stern and not very nice. She won't even look at me. It's like I have a plague or something."

"Maybe that will all change once you and Ed marry and she realizes she will be a grandmother," said Ethel.

"I thought that too, but I'm not too sure. I know she doesn't approve of our age difference, especially since Ed is just out of high school. And what she's not saying is that she disapproves that I've been out of high school for four years already. I think that's all it is, really," said Phyllis.

Ethel said, "Have you tried talking to her about it?"

"I haven't," replied Phyllis, "but Ed has. He keeps asking her to at least try to like me, but she keeps trying to get him to go to college and date someone his own age. I try to get along with her, like that time I practiced 'Amazing Grace' on the piano for weeks, and then when I played it for her, she cut me off halfway through and told me to stop playing *her* piano."

"Yes, I remember you practicing that for her," said Ethel.

"And she won't listen to Ed. Now, here I am, pregnant, and I really should be marrying him sooner than planned, but I can't stand the thought of having her for a mother-in-law. And now Ed and I have been getting into arguments about her." Starting to cry, Phyllis said, "I don't know what to do!"

Ethel hugged her daughter. She was a good listener and knew Phyllis was extremely distressed about her situation. Ethel wished she could do something to help her daughter, but all she could do was support her in her life choices. Phyllis would have to make her own decisions. "About all I can tell you," said Ethel, "is that your relationship with Betty might get better in time, but maybe it won't. It's a decision that you and only you can make. But you now have a third person to think of. I can't tell you what to do, but I can support your decision. If you decide not to marry Ed, then you'll need to make some decisions where your baby is concerned."

Phyllis said, "I understand what you're saying. What you're saying is that I'll need to make the decision to be a single parent, or no parent at all."

That realization hit her hard. She broke down in tears, weeping uncontrollably. Goodness, how had she let it get to this point?

In the next couple of months, Phyllis's hope was that Betty would invite her for Sunday dinner and they would talk things over and make peace with each other. But there was no invitation for dinner, nor an offer to talk things over.

Phyllis and Ed were spending less time together. She didn't sit next to him in his car anymore, and they stopped holding hands. They stopped going to church together. They stopped their marriage classes. They argued over just about everything. Phyllis knew what she had to do.

Phyllis said, "Ed, you and I both know that our wedding needs to be called off, unless you think that your mom will start treating me like her daughter-in-law and our baby like her grandchild."

Ed replied, "I've tried talking to her, you know that. She wants nothing to do with our baby, which I can't understand because I'm the father. The baby has my bloodline. I just don't get it."

"I don't get it either. I'll call Father Brady and tell him to cancel our wedding," said Phyllis. She was shaking as she removed her engagement ring that Ed had so lovingly picked out for her. She placed it in his hand, turned around, and walked away.

Four months into her pregnancy, at the beginning of the new year, Phyllis called Father Brady and canceled their wedding.

"Before I formed you in the womb, I knew you. Before you were born, I set you apart."
—Jeremiah 1:5

6

Phyllis

1955

Pregnant. Phyllis had so many thoughts going through her head, and she wasn't making any sense out of any of them. She was so confused and didn't know which way was up. The only thing she knew for certain was that she valued life and there was no way on this earth she would ever consider abortion and ruled that out immediately. She had seen news stories about doctors performing them illegally, in makeshift offices, and she wanted nothing to do with that. Abortion was in its early days so there were associated deaths and many horror stories going around. With all the crazy things going through her head, she decided to give herself a couple of weeks to calm down and get to thinking straight again.

Phyllis's dream was shattered, and there would be no wedding. Single and pregnant. What was she going to do? She was upset, crying all the time and not wanting to eat, but she knew she had to for the baby's sake. She had to get back into a regular routine. Being the head bookkeeper at her job, she was able to sit all day, which helped tremendously. Her boss allowed her to work through her pregnancy.

The weeks turned into months, and she was in her fifth month. Ed didn't call very often, but Phyllis was glad about that because hearing his voice made her think of what could have been, and then she would cry for two days straight. Now she was facing this pregnancy alone. Thank goodness her family was supportive. She knew she had to start thinking seriously about her plans for her baby. She had so many thoughts going through her head, but the most compelling one was to keep it. Phyllis already was in love with that baby and wanted to raise it by herself.

She also thought about adoption. Should she place her baby with a nice couple to raise? And what kind of adoption—a closed one where there would be no contact at all, or an open one where there is contact with the parents and the child? Did she want to know the adoptive family or not? Which one? So much to consider.

She stopped in to visit her mother and drop off some homemade bread one January day in 1955. Ethel told Phyllis that she had been doing some homework. She said, "Can you stay for a little bit? We can sit at the table here. I have something I want to talk to you about. You might like this."

Phyllis said, "Well, now I'm curious. What do you want to talk to me about?"

Ethel replied, "I found a maternity home in Sioux Falls where unwed pregnant girls can stay throughout their pregnancy, have the baby there, then place the baby for adoption in Sioux Falls. You could take classes or learn a new craft during that time. I think you could continue those classes you started at the college."

"That would be great," replied Phyllis.

Ethel continued, reading the pamphlet, "You'd have your own room, and it looks like the food is good and hot. Three meals, breakfast, lunch, and supper, with snack time allowed in the afternoons. The girls take turns with kitchen duties. There is a community room where you could watch television and a recreation room with pool tables, games, and puzzles. Movie night is every Friday night. They take care of everything from beginning to end."

"Sounds interesting," said Phyllis. "It would be nice to be around other girls who are going through the same thing. I would like that."

"Then, after you had the baby," continued Ethel, "you could return home and pick up where you left off. I have some information here for you to read over. There's a phone number listed in case you have any questions. Read it over and see if this might be something you'd be interested in."

Phyllis looked through the pamphlet and was very interested in what she was reading. "The only thing that worries me about this," said Phyllis, "is that I would have to quit my job and move out of my apartment. I don't want to do either of those. If I can figure out how to keep my job, this would be a wonderful place to go through my pregnancy and have my baby."

"Well, go ahead and study it. You can decide at any time. This would be a good thing to consider. You don't have to make a decision immediately, but the sooner you do, the better, as that would take a load off your shoulders."

This was one of those Florence Crittenton homes that were located in just about every state. The Florence Crittenton Homes Association began in 1950 with the mission to provide a place for unwed pregnant girls to stay while waiting for their babies to be born.

Phyllis was very impressed with her mother. Ethel was looking for an organization that could help Phyllis get through her pregnancy, and she had gone to a lot of trouble to get this information for her. What a neat option. She had no idea there was such a place and couldn't wait to get home to read all about it. She couldn't wait to call her sister and tell her what their mother had found.

There were a few things that weren't mentioned in that pamphlet, however. The maternity home had some strict rules. The primary purpose for the home was to house pregnant girls until they gave birth and then surrendered the baby for adoption. The girls were not to get comfortable and were supposed to look forward to returning home. The maternity home looked like an institution. Cold. Unwelcoming. The brochure made it sound like it was comfortable, serving delicious meals and having daily activities to keep the girls busy while they waited to have their babies. A home away from home. But in reality, it was a place to hide their shame from their family and friends. The home protected them until they could reenter their lives in their hometowns. But the rules and the layers of secrecy were so harsh that the girls were being shamed. One of those rules was that the girls would be given an assumed name, their real names kept secret. They were not allowed to ask questions of one another, and they were not to make friends. This would not fit Phyllis at all. She was a social butterfly, and every person she met became her friend. She would have wanted to be friends with every one of those girls. Of course, since this was left out of the brochure, neither Phyllis nor Ethel knew these rules.

If Phyllis wanted to go out to a movie, she would have to go in a group, and they would each have to put on a fake wedding band first. Phyllis's parents could come over and take her out for lunch once a week, but they would be the only company allowed. Communication was strictly monitored, and letters coming in and going out were censored. Absolutely no contact was allowed with the father of the baby. These rules were kept very strict during the fifties because society didn't know how to handle this problem. In the next decades, the rules lightened up considerably.

Also, Ethel would not be able to go inside and help Phyllis get settled in, nor would she be able to be with her at the hospital. Actually, no one would be with her. One of the house workers would accompany Phyllis to the hospital, but only to the door. After that, she would be on her own. No information about the labor or delivery was given to the girls, so they had no idea what to expect. This rule was especially harsh. Had Ethel known about *all* of their rules, she may not have promoted the home so energetically to Phyllis. The girls weren't treated with respect at all. If anything, they were treated with disdain on purpose because they were pregnant and unmarried, the baby being "illegitimate," a word that was whispered in someone's ear, not to be said out loud.

The social workers determined that the problem with pregnancies out of wedlock was a psychological one, making the girls unfit to raise children. They would tell the girls that, if they chose to keep their babies, the child would be called a bastard on the playground, which would be an awful thing to put a child through. There was only one choice, the social workers deemed, and that was to surrender the baby for adoption. The girls were coerced into handing over their babies to adoption agencies without being informed of their legal rights. People looked down their noses at unwed pregnant women.

Following the birth of the baby, Phyllis could decide if she wanted to hold the baby, and feed and change it. If so, she could do so for ten days. Then on the tenth day, Phyllis would have to decide if she wanted to keep her baby or say her goodbyes as the baby would be surrendered and she would have to sign the papers for adoption. She could name her baby whatever she wanted, and under the heading "Father" would be the word *Unknown*.

Almost all of the birth certificates of babies surrendered in this time period had "Unknown" on them. This way the identity of the father was kept secret and he would be in the clear with nothing to worry about. He could go on with his life. Nowadays, that doesn't happen, and both parents are named on the birth certificate. Naming both parents indicates that the responsibility for the child's upbringing is twofold, and the father is held accountable in helping to provide for his child. Legislation was introduced in the early 1960s to help families with single mothers with food stamps. Welfare (or financial assistance) was yet unheard of.

The pamphlet in hand, knowing only what was printed on it, but not the strict rules that were conveniently left out of it, Phyllis decided to think seriously about going to live there. After visiting with her mother, she headed to Dorothy's house. She couldn't wait to talk to her about this place.

"Dorothy," said Phyllis excitedly, "look what Mom gave me. She was doing some research on unwed pregnant girls and found this place in Sioux Falls. She called them to get some information and they sent this to her. I think I like it. This place would be great for me."

Dorothy was sitting at the kitchen table, giving her baby a bottle. Phyllis handed her the pamphlet to read. Dorothy looked it over and said, "It looks nice. Where is it again?"

"Sioux Falls," replied Phyllis. "That's the only thing I don't like about it, because I'm pretty sure I'd have to quit my job, and I don't want to do that. I'd have to move out of my apartment too, but I'm not worried about that. There'll be other apartments available when I return home." She reached over and took the baby from Dorothy as he was done eating. Phyllis held him and rocked him in her arms.

"I guess you could ask your boss if he would hold your job for you until you get back. It doesn't hurt to ask anyway." Dorothy picked up the pamphlet and looked at it closer, turning it over after she read the front part. "Yeah, I think you would like it there."

Phyllis laid the baby in his cradle, the same cradle she laid in as a baby, with her brothers making faces at her. This memory brought a smile to her face.

Phyllis and her niece Delores had been spending a lot of time together the past few years, going to movies and shopping. Delores visited Phyllis at her apartment often, and on one of her visits, they talked about the home for unwed mothers. Sitting in the living room one day, watching *The Ed Sullivan Show*, Phyllis showed Delores the pamphlet. She looked it over.

Delores said, "What do you think of the place, Phyllis? It sounds pretty neat."

"Yeah, I think so too. If my boss will hold my job until I get back, I will probably move over there in a month or so."

The calendar changed over to February 1955. Phyllis was concentrating on work and her family, spending many hours with her parents and with Dorothy and Delores. Dorothy was a big help for Phyllis in keeping her head on straight and making sure she was eating properly. Dorothy had just given birth to son number two in November, so she had a lot of maternity clothes for Phyllis to borrow. Phyllis had fun going through her sister's closet again. She got by pretty well with those clothes and didn't have to buy very much. She spent a lot of time at Dorothy's house, watching *I Love Lucy* and helping her with her newborn son, feeding him and changing his diapers. She was secretly getting some practice in and ideas on how to care for a baby. She was also secretly thinking about keeping her baby.

Phyllis approached her boss one day in February and asked him if he would be willing to hold her job open so she could stay at the Home for Unwed Mothers in Sioux Falls until her baby was born.

Her boss replied, "I can't do that, Phyllis. I need a bookkeeper and I'd have to fill that position. But I do have an option that might work for you. If you'd like, you can work here through your pregnancy and you can take more breaks if needed. We can work with you on that."

Wow, Phyllis was speechless at that offer. She had no idea she was that appreciated by her boss. She did like her job and the people she worked with. She had much to think about.

During the fifties, many of the girls who were pregnant didn't know the first thing about sex education. There was nothing taught in school or by their parents. They knew nothing about pregnancy, why they were getting bigger, or what was going to happen during delivery. Some didn't even know that it took nine months. A lot of girls were clueless.

Dorothy had helped their mother raise Phyllis. Ethel and Dorothy were the two most influential women in Phyllis's life. They were her advisors. During her developing years, they both helped her with buying her first bra, and they showed her how to wear menstrual pads and explained how periods worked. Phyllis was very close with her dad too, but he couldn't answer these kinds of questions. These were left to the women. Phyllis was very lucky to have Dorothy around, because she was a little more up to date on the latest information on things that Phyllis questioned. Dorothy was especially helpful when it came to pregnancy and childbirth and taught her everything Phyllis would need to know about pregnancy.

One day early on in Phyllis's pregnancy, she asked Dorothy,

"What's it like being pregnant? Will I have weird cravings like you did?"

"Probably, and I can't wait to see what your cravings will be! But you have to remember that you're eating for two, so you need to eat healthy foods like fruits and vegetables," said Dorothy. "Let's see, what else can I tell you? You'll get a little bigger each week of course. The skin around your stomach area will stretch some, and make marks, but if you rub lotion on it, it'll help soften those stretch marks."

"Oh, I didn't know that. I'd better get some good lotion. I'll pick some up at the drugstore on my way home." Phyllis made a mental note to do that. "How do you know when it's time to go to the hospital?"

"Oh, you'll know when it's time. You'll have some contraction pains that will last for a few seconds. You'll know that pain. It'll stop you in your tracks. And when your water breaks, it's definitely time. You'll know that when you see a puddle on the floor."

"Oh fun, can't wait," said Phyllis, feeling squeamish.

Phyllis and Dorothy had many discussions about what she was going to do after the baby's birth. Phyllis was secretly thinking about keeping the baby, but she decided to keep quiet about that for the time being. In the meantime, Phyllis kept up with work, shopping occasionally and going to movies with Delores. She knew that people were talking about her behind her back because she would catch them looking at her from time to time. But she didn't care. She kept her head up and trudged on.

Phyllis was still thinking about that home in Sioux Falls.

She was spending her lunch break at Dorothy's house one day, and they were having another conversation about the home in Sioux Falls. Phyllis said, "I've been thinking a lot about that lately. I really love Mitchell. My family and friends are here, and I don't want to leave. In addition, I have the best boss ever, and he's willing to keep me on through the pregnancy. He's even giving me extra breaks if I need them. I'm thinking I might stay in Mitchell, but I haven't made a definite decision about it yet."

"Yes, you do have a wonderful boss. I can't argue with that. Whatever you decide, I'm behind you one-hundred percent," said Dorothy.

One Saturday in March, Phyllis was at the drugstore on Main Street, picking up some lotion, when Mr. Smith, the pharmacist, got Phyllis's attention and waved her over to the pharmacy. He asked, "Phyllis, do you have a few minutes to talk?"

"Sure," replied Phyllis, puzzled, thinking, *I wonder what this is about.*

Mr. Smith had been the pharmacist at the drugstore ever since he graduated from pharmacy school. He was in his thirties, married, and originally from Mitchell. He was very lucky to be able to step in and run his own pharmacy after the previous pharmacist retired. He was tall, with dark hair and glasses. He had a loud voice, which he could project into the store to call the customers over to pick up their medicine. His customers liked him very much, and he would often ask how their families were doing. He remembered their names too. He was very personable.

Mr. Smith asked Phyllis to have a seat at the consultation table. He took the chair across from her and said, "Thank you for taking this time to chat with me. How are you doing?"

Phyllis replied, "I'm doing all right so far. I've got about three more months left before I have this baby." What was he wanting? She was very curious.

"Could I get you a bottle of pop?" asked Mr. Smith, feeling nervous.

"Sure," Phyllis said, still puzzled. "I could go for a cherry Coke or grape Nehi."

He brought two bottles of cherry Coke to the table. "May I ask what your plans are for your baby? Do you know yet?"

Phyllis replied, "No, not yet, but I do have some options to consider."

"I have another option for you to think about. You don't have to give me an answer right away. This is something that is going to require some thought."

Phyllis said, "All right, what is the option you're talking about?"

"Well," said the pharmacist, cautiously, "hear me out, okay?" He paused for a moment. "My wife and I cannot have children, and we would love to adopt your baby. We'd be great parents. I'm sorry to spring this on you here in the store. If you would be willing to visit with my wife and me together, you could come over to our house and we could talk more there."

Phyllis replied, "That would be all right, but I'm not ready just yet. Right now, I'm confused and not ready to make any decisions. The next time I come in, though, I'll stop over and talk to you about it, maybe meet with you and your wife one evening."

Mr. Smith replied, "That's wonderful. I just wanted to let you know that there is another option. And it's a good one, as the baby would have nice clothes, good schooling, his or her own room, a big family, and good food. The baby would have lots of cousins and aunts and uncles. I travel sometimes for conferences and could take the family along for a vacation. Please think about this and call anytime if you have any questions."

"Okay, I will," said Phyllis, her head spinning. She wanted to get out of there.

Mr. Smith continued, "If you wanted to, you could opt for an open adoption. That way you could have a part in your baby's life. We'd be good with that." He took a drink of his pop. "Please consider us. We'd be great parents for your little one." He was relieved to finally get that out, as he had been trying to get the courage to say something for about a month. "Thank you for hearing me out."

Phyllis thanked him for the pop and promised him that she would sincerely think about it. She headed for Dorothy's house immediately to tell her about this conversation.

"Dorothy, you're not going to believe this!" exclaimed Phyllis. "I just came from the drugstore, and Mr. Smith, the pharmacist, asked if I had plans for my baby yet."

Dorothy said, "Really? Why did he do that?"

Phyllis continued, "He said that he had another option for me to consider. He said that he and his wife can't have children, and they would like to adopt my baby. He wants me to come over to their house to talk to them about it. Dorothy, I couldn't get out of there fast enough. I don't know why that bothered me so much, but it did. I'm just not ready to think about that yet."

"There's no need to rush into it right now," said Dorothy. "When you feel more ready to talk it over with them, then give them a call." She went to the kitchen to check on her cookies that were in the oven. "But really, this *is* a good option. But would you be agreeable to knowing where your child is all the time?"

"I don't know. Mr. Smith did say that I could decide on an open adoption and that way I could have a part in my child's life," said Phyllis.

"Hmm, how do you feel about that? Would your child remind you of Ed? I see both pros and cons to this, the pro being that our family would know your child. I would love that, and so would Mom and Dad. But we're not the ones who need to make this monumental decision."

"Yeah, I do have a lot of thinking to do. I would like to put this all behind me and get on with my life. I wouldn't be able to make a clean break if the Smiths adopt my baby."

Oh boy, now her head was really swimming. There were so many decisions to make and not much time left. Ed called once in a great while to see if she needed anything, as he felt an obligation to see this through with Phyllis. She appreciated it, but it sure did hurt hearing his voice. She was angry with him and loved him at the same time. She was anxious to have her baby and to get Ed out of her life for good.

Phyllis kept going back and forth, thinking about that

home in Sioux Falls. She eventually decided against it once and for all. She loved her job and loved having good friends and family who supported her, and she was unable to bring herself to leave Mitchell. Her mom was very supportive and understood her reasoning for not wanting to go to Sioux Falls. She reminded Phyllis that her parents were both behind her every step of the way. Phyllis faced this head on.

Besides her parents, Dorothy was Phyllis's biggest supporter, as well as her advisor, throughout her pregnancy. They spent a lot of time together, talking about pregnancy and babies. Phyllis said, "Dorothy, I've been thinking about keeping my baby and raising it myself. I don't want to go to the home in Sioux Falls, and I'm leaning against the Smiths' offer to adopt my baby."

Dorothy replied, "Phyllis, I know you mean well and you already love that baby, but really, it needs a mother *and* a father. You can't raise a baby on your own with what you earn at work. What would you do if your baby was sick?"

Phyllis replied, "Yes, I do love this baby very much. I make a pretty good salary at my job, so I think I could manage it. And if my baby was sick, I would take a vacation day off."

"The biggest question of all," said Dorothy, "is who is going to watch your child while you're at work? I've got four children, two of them little ones, so I wouldn't be able to take care of a baby in addition to my four. And Mom and Dad are getting up there in years. They would have a tough time of it, especially when your little one starts walking."

"But Dorothy," said Phyllis, "How about if Mom and Dad take care of my child for two days a week, you for one day, and then that just leaves two more days. Would that work, do you think?"

"Maybe, but there's one more thing," said Dorothy. "You would lose your independence. You wouldn't be able to just hop in the car and go somewhere like you usually do. Also, you can forget about going to movies on the weekends."

"I'll have to think about it and come up with a solution," said Phyllis, frustrated.

During the fifties, there was no such thing as day care yet. It was very uncommon for a single woman to be raising a baby on her own, unless she was a widow. And a widow was able to get financial assistance, but not a single woman with a baby.

Phyllis thought about this a lot, so much that it was making her head spin, and she was going "this way and that way" about it. She knew Dorothy was right; she was the voice of reason. She couldn't raise her baby on her own; it would have been a struggle. She didn't want to have to ask her parents and siblings to babysit or for money to pay a babysitter, if she could even find one. Deep down, Phyllis knew she couldn't keep her baby.

A week later, Phyllis went over to Dorothy's house to tell her she had made a decision. "Dorothy," she said, "I've decided not to keep my baby. The conversation we had last week hit me like a brick. You're right, I can't expect family to babysit my child while I'm at work. And you're right about me losing my independence too. It would be very hard to raise a baby on my own."

"Oh, Phyllis, I know you've been going back and forth on that subject for a couple of months. There's nothing I'd like more than to know my niece or nephew, but I also agree that you made the right decision."

Toward the end of March, as Phyllis was in her seventh month of pregnancy, she had to go to the drugstore to make a purchase. She hoped to avoid the pharmacist because she still hadn't made up her mind about that situation. She wasn't too sure if she even wanted an open adoption, or if she wanted to know who was raising her child. So, Phyllis thought she would just pop in, get what she needed, and pay for it quick and get out. She was at the checkout when a voice behind her said, "Hi, Phyllis, when you get done there, can you stop over at the pharmacy for a minute or two?" It was Mr. Smith.

Phyllis knew that he was going to want an update on where she was with her pregnancy.

"I just thought I'd check in with you and see how you're doing and if you've made any decisions yet," said Mr. Smith.

Phyllis replied, "Mr. Smith, I haven't made a decision on what we talked about yet. I'm going back and forth on the open adoption part of it. I'm not sure how I feel about knowing where my child is."

"I understand," said Mr. Smith. "Whatever decision you make, my wife and I will respect it."

People were getting on her nerves, and she wished they'd stop telling her what to do. She was annoyed, and it showed. This was out of character for her, but she knew people were talking about her behind her back, and it was starting to get to her. She didn't like it. It was mean. She made herself ignore it because, after all, she was the one who had decided to stay in Mitchell throughout her pregnancy, and she would hold her head up high. It was getting closer to delivery time, and she still didn't know what she wanted to do about the pharmacist. She had to decide soon if she wanted an open adoption or a closed adoption.

It was springtime in Mitchell, the end of April 1955. Phyllis was eight months pregnant, and it was getting down to the wire. Just one month to go and it would all be over. So much had happened.

She stopped over to visit her parents on that last day of April and brought them each a May basket that she had made. A May basket is a small basket holding a gift such as flowers or candy, given to friends and family on May Day (May 1). She would take some baskets to Dorothy and Delores and to her other siblings. She said, "Mom, I think I know what I'm going to do now. I'm going to place my baby for adoption, and it will be a closed adoption. For a long time, I thought about Mr. and Mrs. Smith and how badly they want to adopt. The only thing I didn't like about that arrangement is that I would know where my baby was at all times, and I would much rather not know. What do you think about that decision?"

Her mother said, "I believe you've made the right decision. I feel so sad for the pharmacist and his wife, but this is the best option for you and your baby."

And with that, her decision was final. It would be a closed adoption. Now to tell the Smiths. Phyllis decided to go over to their house to talk to them. This was going to be difficult, but she didn't want to deliver that news to the pharmacist at the drugstore. Oh, she dreaded this. She called their phone number and asked if she could come over the next day, Sunday, in the afternoon. They settled on one o'clock.

On Sunday at one o'clock, Phyllis was shaking as she drove up to the Smiths' house and exited her car. She rang the doorbell, and they welcomed her in. She presented each of them with a May basket.

Mrs. Smith asked, "Would you like something to drink? We have orange juice and cherry Coke."

Phyllis replied, "No, thank you." Normally, she'd jump on the cherry Coke, but her stomach was a bit queasy.

"Come on in and have a seat anywhere in the living room," said Mrs. Smith. "How have you been feeling? Is your pregnancy pretty normal so far?"

"Yes, I've been seeing my doctor regularly, in another town, and he says that things are progressing nicely. Anyway, I just wanted to stop by and talk to you both about the conversation we had about adoption."

"Yes," said Mr. Smith. "Have you made a decision about your baby yet?"

Phyllis replied, "Yes, I have." The pharmacist and his wife were wonderful people, and they would be terribly disappointed to hear her decision. Her heart was racing, and her stomach was queasy. She wanted to get this over with.

Tearfully, Phyllis said, "I've decided to place my baby for adoption, but it will be a closed adoption. The reason being that I don't want to know where my baby is going, and I don't want to find myself driving down your street to get a glimpse of him or her." Her hands were shaking. "That's why I have decided against an open adoption. It has nothing to do with you. I know you would be great parents."

"We understand your position, really we do," said Mr. Smith. "We're disappointed, of course, but when we visited the last time, and I mentioned an open adoption, it didn't seem to interest you, so I kind of expected you to choose the closed adoption."

"I did think long and hard on that," said Phyllis, crying. "The other options I had were much easier for me to figure out than this one. I prayed for the answer to this question. You probably already know that Ed and I broke up and that we canceled our wedding. I need to make a clean break and get on with my life."

Mrs. Smith said, "Oh, Phyllis, I can't imagine all you've been through. And to think that you've gone through this alone. I'm glad you have your family here and that you're close. Take care of yourself in this last month of your pregnancy."

Phyllis replied, "I will, thank you. I want you to know that I am so sorry, and I pray that you are able to adopt very soon. You would be great parents."

"Thank you, Phyllis," said Mr. Smith. "This wasn't the news we were hoping for, but we understand your decision."

Phyllis was relieved to be out of there and back in her car. It had gone much better than she thought it would. They were so nice to her, and they weren't too upset about her decision. They had already been expecting the answer to be no. She had gone in there shaking and dreading being there but came out relieved.

She made the rounds from Dorothy's house to Delores's

house and then her parents' house and told them all about the meeting with the pharmacist and his wife. "Dorothy," said Phyllis, "they are so nice. Their house is beautiful, and it smelled like roast beef in there. I felt comfortable around them. When I first got there, my stomach was queasy and I was shaky, but that didn't last long. They made me feel at home."

Dorothy replied, "You did the right thing. I was thinking about you. I know it had to be a difficult thing to do."

Everyone agreed that Phyllis made the right decision with the closed adoption. They would keep the Smiths in their prayers every day. Dorothy, Delores, and Ethel were all pleased to know that Phyllis would place her baby for adoption. While Dorothy would have liked nothing better than to have a new niece or nephew, she knew Phyllis would have many struggles with raising a child on her own.

To pass the time, Phyllis continued on with her normal routine. Getting up to go to work every morning, buying groceries, shopping on Saturday, church on Sunday, and visiting her family regularly kept her on track. Even though she and Ed had called off their wedding, she remained Catholic as she loved the Catholic faith and chose to stay at Holy Family Church. She felt welcome there. The church accepted her as she was. She respected the Catholic Church teachings and Father Brady.

Planning ahead, Phyllis met with an attorney from Catholic Adoptions to draw up adoption papers so that all would be ready to go when the baby was born. With a closed adoption, all names and addresses would be covered up at the time of signing. Phyllis would name the baby, and the papers would be filed under that name. She had names picked out for both a boy and a girl. She would get to fill out a birth certificate with that name. She knew the name she picked would only be for ten days. After that, the baby's adoptive parents would give it a different name. And she was okay with that. There had to be a birth certificate for every baby, thus creating a paper trail.

Phyllis stipulated that her baby be placed in a Catholic home.

"Do you want
to do something
beautiful for God?
There is a person
who needs you. This
is your chance."
—Mother Teresa

7

Jack and Marion

(THE ADOPTIVE PARENTS)

Jack Pershing Steckelberg was born in Chamberlain, South Dakota, in 1918 and was the fourth of eight children. He grew up on the family farm, following in his father's and grandfather's footsteps. He was tall and muscular and had a permanent tan from working on the farm. He came from a long line of German immigrants, his great-grandparents leading the way, sailing on a ship to America. He served in the US Army during World War II in North Africa and Italy. He was the fourth generation of Steckelbergs to worship at the Congregational church in Chamberlain.

Marion Margaret Moore was born in 1918 in Pukwana, South Dakota, the first of two children; her brother would be born two years later. She graduated with a teaching degree from Notre Dame Junior College in Mitchell, which was associated with Holy Family Church. Upon graduation, she taught at a school just north of Chamberlain. All twelve grades shared the same room. Marion was a good teacher, and she would have lifelong friendships with her students. She came from a long line of Irish Catholic immigrants, the Bradys. They were a close-knit family, and most of her ancestors settled in the Pukwana area.

Jack and Marion were married in 1946 upon Jack's arrival home from his war service overseas and upon his conversion to the Catholic faith, which was necessary to marry in the Catholic Church. The two immediately settled into the life of farming in the Chamberlain area. Marion jumped right in with the cooking, cleaning, and canning, and she helped Jack with whatever she could on the farm. They talked about starting a family right away. Their evening prayers included a request for a son or daughter.

But for some reason, their prayers had gone unanswered. Weeks went by, then months, and no pregnancy. Their doctors found nothing wrong. Their disappointment grew, but they realized that it must be God's will.

Father McPhillips was their priest, and he came out to the farm often to visit and to pray with them. He had been the priest for the Chamberlain and Pukwana churches for several years, and everyone in the area loved him. Born in Alabama, Father Mac, as he was called, had just a touch of that southern drawl to his voice. He was tall, handsome, and clean shaven, and his voice was pleasant and soothing. To say that he was friendly and congenial, with a healthy sense of humor, described him perfectly. He loved the people of these two towns; on the weekends, he cheered on the sports teams, and during the week, he was an active participant in quite a few of the school activities.

On Sundays, he could be found at the Pukwana and Chamberlain Catholic churches, saying mass at nine o'clock in Pukwana and ten thirty in Chamberlain. Wednesdays were reserved for Catechism, a religion class.

The Catholic faith was the foundation of the Catholic family, and Father Mac called on his parishioners often to ask if they needed anything that the Church could help with and prayed with them. He had been praying with Jack and Marion for several months for divine intervention in starting a family, so on one of his visits, he brought up the subject of adoption.

Father Mac said, "The Catholic church has a new program for childless couples, called Catholic Adoptions. There are some women in the state who are unmarried and expecting a baby, and they have chosen not to marry the father. They have made the decision to place their babies for adoption. This seems to be happening all over the country. Unfortunately, the numbers of these babies are increasing, which is concerning."

Marion asked, "Are you saying the mothers are giving up their own babies willingly? That's hard to believe."

"Yes, some of the girls are very young and can't provide for a baby nor are they ready for marriage. They want to do the right thing and give their baby to a couple who will raise it as their own," replied Father Mac.

"I've never heard of such a thing," said Marion. "Do they mind giving their babies away?"

Father Mac replied, "They are unwed, and the mother realizes that her child deserves so much more than what she can give."

Marion and Jack had never heard of a mother raising children alone. It wasn't something that was done.

Marion replied, "I just can't understand it. Why are there so many girls that are pregnant out of wedlock? I have a hard time believing that they would just give their babies away."

"It's happening all over the country now. Some of the girls are very young, in their early teens, pregnant, and they are in no position to be raising a baby. These babies are then having to be placed for adoption."

"Are there quite a few babies available? And are all of the girls Catholic?" asked Jack.

"There aren't a lot of babies available through Catholic Charities because we are a private adoption group. There are other adoption agencies that would have more babies available for adoption, but the mothers of the babies through Catholic Charities are themselves Catholic," said Father Mac. "One other thing: for you, there is no cost going through Catholic Charities, since you are of the Catholic faith."

As Catholics, knowing that the child would be in the faith was important to them, almost like knowing beforehand they would fit right into the family. It made it easier for Marion to consider adoption and to understand the feelings of the birth mother. After all, wouldn't she want her baby raised in a good Catholic home?

"Is there a waiting list? If so, how long is the wait?" asked Marion.

"Yes, there's a waiting list, but the wait depends on the

babies being available and where your name is on the list. Your application will cover the eastern South Dakota diocese, which includes Sioux Falls and Mitchell."

"All right," Jack replied, "Marion and I will talk it over, and we'll let you know what we decide. It gives us comfort that we'd be going through our church instead of through a regular adoption agency."

Father Mac said, "This would be an answer to your prayers of having the family you dreamed about. I'll leave some adoption information with you to read over. We'll talk more about this in a week or so. Let's pray."

Father Mac prayed with them, then he left. Jack and Marion were smiling. They read the adoption information together and decided to talk to their attorney to get his opinion on adoption. They especially wanted to make sure that once they adopted, the baby couldn't be taken away.

Marion called their attorney right away the next morning and scheduled an appointment for the next week. She gave him a brief explanation that it was regarding adoption.

The next week, they arrived at the attorney's office, which was decorated in South Dakota destinations, such as Mount Rushmore, the Corn Palace, and the falls of the Big Sioux River in the city of Sioux Falls. Jack and Marion sat in the chairs opposite his desk. "So, you're interested in adoption?" he asked.

"Yes, we have some questions we'd like to have answers to before we commit to the adoption application. Mainly, we need to know if placing a baby with us would be permanent, or if the mother could change her mind at the last minute," Jack said.

"It depends on the type of adoption you're wanting," said the attorney.

"What do you mean, *type* of adoption?" asked Marion.

The attorney continued, "There are two types—open or closed adoption. Open is where all parties involved can have contact with the child and each other. You would be able to call the mother on the phone, and she could come over and see the child regularly. A closed adoption is where there is no contact at all with the mother. And she would have no contact with the child or the couple adopting her child. All identification for all parties is kept secret."

Jack and Marion were private people, and they didn't want to have to share their baby with anyone else. "A closed adoption is the one we'd prefer," said Jack. Marion nodded her head in agreement.

"It is getting more common for young unmarried women to place their babies for adoption. It's up to the mother to decide if she wants an open adoption or a closed adoption. After the birth, the mother would be given ten days to finalize the adoption. During this time, she may decide to keep her baby. This rarely happens though."

"That would be horrible," said Marion. "For us, at least. I guess it just depends on the mother, if she has the means to provide for her baby or not, or if she decides to marry the father."

The attorney continued, "Exactly. Once the mother decides to place her baby for adoption, you would then be able to get your new son or daughter on the eleventh day after the birth. The baby would be yours, and you could pick out a name of your choosing for him or her. The signing of the adoption papers will take place on that day also."

"What does it cost to adopt?" asked Jack.

"If you decide to adopt through the Catholic Church, there is no charge, except for what the attorney would charge to draw up the adoption papers, and that is usually no charge," replied the attorney.

"No charge!" exclaimed Jack. "Why wouldn't the attorney charge anything?" Jack and Marion couldn't believe there was no charge, but since they hadn't done this before, they didn't know what to expect. They exchanged glances, excited. Sitting in this office made it seem very real.

"Catholic Charities has its own attorney, and since you're Catholic, there is no charge," said the attorney. "Most people give a donation to the church in place of attorney fees."

"Okay. That's what we'll do then. Thank you for your help today. We learned a lot," said Jack.

"I'll send along some information with you about adoption. You may have already seen some of it that the church gave you. I wish you all the best. If there's anything I can help with, just let me know. I would love to help you two become a family," said the attorney.

Jack and Marion left the office, grinning from ear to ear, and headed for home. On the way there, they discussed what their attorney told them.

Marion said, "I like the Catholic Adoptions program, and I think this would be our chance at starting a family."

Jack agreed. "Yes, I think so too. Let's talk to Father Mac after church on Sunday, and we'll find out what we need to do to begin the application process."

Jack and Marion had much to think about, and they continued their nightly prayers for a son or daughter for their family. It was looking like adoption was their only hope of having the family they had been dreaming of.

Following church that Sunday, heading out the front door, Jack and Marion approached Father Mac. They shook his hand, and Jack said, "Let's get started on that application!" This brought huge smiles to all three faces.

"That is the best news I've heard today!" said Father Mac.

Their prayers now included the birth mother and their future son or daughter.

The whole week was spent visiting family members to relay the news that they had filed an application for adoption through the Catholic Church. Their family and friends were excited to hear this news. Lots of prayers were said during this time, and those prayers were for Jack and Marion, the birth mother, and her baby.

Father Mac met with them weekly to fill out paperwork and applications and to discuss the process of adoption. One very important part of this process was to have a home inspection by a social worker to make sure that the baby would have a good and safe home environment. The home inspection was performed by the social worker, a nice young lady. There were several items on the list to be checked off, including cupboard space, table, highchair, baby bedroom, and so forth. All the boxes were checked, and the inspection was deemed successful. The social worker sat down at the table with Jack and Marion for an hour going over the application, which was then transferred to the office of Catholic Charities.

Then, they waited. In the meantime, Jack worked on the farm, hunted, and fished, and Marion continued calling on the farm ladies in the area, baking bread, and gathering the eggs. She kept the house spotless in case of a surprise inspection, although it was always that way anyway.

In the spring of 1955, Father Brady from Mitchell contacted Father Mac with the news that one of his parishioners, a single woman, was expecting and would be placing the baby for adoption. The birth mother specified that the adoptive couple be Catholic. Father Brady knew that Father Mac had been working with a couple in Pukwana and felt that they would be a good match. Whether Father Mac told Father Brady it was Jack and Marion wanting to adopt is unknown, Marion being Father Brady's cousin and all. They took that knowledge to the grave. The baby's due date was the end of May or the beginning of June.

Father Mac made a special trip that spring to see Jack and Marion. "I have some good news to tell you. There is a woman at Holy Family Church in Mitchell who is expecting. She was engaged to be married, but unfortunately, they have decided to call off their wedding. She is going to place her baby for adoption, as she feels that would be the best thing for all parties involved."

Jack and Marion both teared up. "This is an answer to prayer, but I'm sad for the birth mother. She must be devastated," said Marion. "I just can't imagine what she's going through."

They relayed the news of a baby available for adoption to their families only, as this was a sad time for the mother for the sacrifice she was making.

The prospect of being parents excited and thrilled the couple. The weekly meetings and prayers continued with Father Mac. There would be another home inspection. Jack and Marion continued with their normal daily routine and farm chores. Every day, they prayed for the birth mother, thankful to her for making this very difficult decision and for allowing them to adopt her baby. Though Marion didn't carry this baby physically, she was tied to it emotionally. She imagined what it was like to be pregnant and felt every emotion. Their dream of having a son or daughter was finally coming true. This was the greatest gift—and the greatest sacrifice—any mother could give. They were counting down the days to the birth of their baby. Would it be a boy or a girl? Nobody would know until the baby was born as there were no tests available to determine the sex at that time.

"It's a girl!" said the nurse.
"Do you want to hold her?"
"No," replied the patient.
"I wish I could, but it's best that I don't. It would break my heart. Take her away immediately, please."
Phyllis heard her baby cry, and it about tore her apart.

8

Phyllis

Very early on Tuesday morning, May 31, 1955, Phyllis started having contractions. Her parents were out of state at the time, so she called Dorothy in a panic. "Dorothy! I think it's time! I'm having contractions! Hurry!"

The two sisters had already arranged ahead of time for Phyllis to call when it was time. Phyllis was all ready to go when Dorothy drove up. She helped Phyllis into the car, and the two of them headed for the hospital. Upon arrival at the emergency entrance, the hospital personnel came out and helped Phyllis into a wheelchair and whisked her inside while Dorothy parked the car. Phyllis had already called her doctor from home, and he met her there. She also called Ed and told him she was going to the hospital.

Phyllis was taken to the maternity ward for monitoring. Dorothy was there to help her keep calm and to hold her hand when she had a contraction. Finally, the doctor sent her to the delivery room. Phyllis's labor went smoothly, and her doctor delivered a healthy baby girl at 8:20 a.m., weighing six pounds, fifteen ounces.

"It's a girl!" said the nurse. "Do you want to hold her?"

"No," replied the patient. "I wish I could, but it's best that I don't. It would break my heart. Take her away immediately, please." Saying that took every ounce of strength she had left. Phyllis heard her baby cry, and it about tore her apart. She didn't want to see her for fear that she would change her mind and keep her. Phyllis had made her decision, and there was no going back.

The nurse then asked, "Do you want to name her?"

"Yes," said Phyllis. "Kathryn Lynn Cunningham is her name." She spelled out the names for the nurse. It took strength and selflessness to want a better life for her child.

Dorothy was glad that Phyllis had an easy delivery and that the baby was healthy, but Phyllis would be going home empty-handed. On top of it all, she had to stay in the hospital for an entire week in the maternity ward, hearing the babies cry, one of them her own daughter. Dorothy was heartbroken for her sister.

Phyllis's parents had been out of state visiting family, but they drove all night and returned home the next day. They went to the hospital immediately to see her. Two days later, Ethel asked Phyllis, "Would it be all right with you if I could hold your baby and spend a little time with her?"

Phyllis said, "Yes, but in another room. I don't want to see or hear either of you." The nurse took Ethel to an empty room, then went to the nursery to get the baby. Nobody knows how long the two were in the room together or what was said. Phyllis didn't ask, and Ethel didn't tell. One can only imagine—the I love yous and wishes for a happy, healthy life.

Phyllis's emotions were all over the place. Her room was the farthest away from the nursery. She was glad about that. She kept her door shut so she wouldn't have to see the people walking by with their new babies. Being in the maternity ward for an entire week just about tore her up. This was quite possibly the hardest thing for her to go through.

Phyllis's attorney brought the adoption papers later that week for her to sign, and he had to give her the news that there was a couple wanting to adopt her baby girl and that they were Catholic. Many, many tears were shed in that hospital room, but it gave her time to think things through. She had many heart-to-heart talks with family members during that hospital stay. It's difficult to understand the level of strength and courage Phyllis had in that situation.

She stayed with her parents for a couple of weeks to heal and get back to her normal self. Taking that time off from work allowed her to regroup. June 10 was a particularly rough day, as that was the day her baby's new parents came to get her. The attorney didn't give any details as to the location. Phyllis was okay with that; she just made sure to keep her mind off of it that day by going on a shopping trip to get some new clothes—some shopping therapy.

Phyllis remembered every detail of the delivery of the baby girl that she would never see or hold. She had carried her baby girl for the full nine months, and she was emotionally invested in her. She agonized for weeks over the fate of her baby. She would have been able and eager to raise her daughter had things turned out differently with Ed. In the end, the decision was made to place her baby with a Catholic couple.

Upon leaving the hospital, Phyllis had a horrible, empty feeling for weeks and wondered constantly if she did the right thing. Her answer was usually yes. But goodness, she hoped this agonizing feeling would go away soon.

She sobbed when confronted with the adoption papers, knowing she was saying goodbye to her daughter forever. She was distraught and depressed for weeks after, praying to God to take the awful feelings away. She found herself looking at every baby she saw and wondering, *Could she be my baby girl Kathryn?*

Phyllis didn't place her baby for adoption because she didn't love her. On the contrary, she did it because she loved this precious baby girl so much and wanted only the best for her.

Gradually, day by day, she was able to get back to a semblance of her old self. She went back to work and back to her apartment. On one of her shopping trips, she purchased a new handbag in which she carried a small calendar. In the May 31 block, she wrote "Kathryn Lynn Cunningham," and her nightly prayers now included Kathryn Lynn.

"Not flesh of my flesh,
Nor bone of my bone,
But still miraculously my own.
Never forget for a single minute,
You didn't grow under my heart,
But in it."
—Fleur Conkling Heyliger

9

Jack and Marion

Father Mac called Marion in the afternoon of May 31 to ask if she and Jack would be home later on. He had some great news. Marion said, "Yes, come out in an hour." Marion walked out to the barn and told Jack that Father Mac was coming over in an hour with great news. Jack came in and cleaned up.

Upon arrival at the farm, Father Mac announced, "A healthy baby girl was born at St. Joseph's Hospital in Mitchell at 8:20 a.m. this morning, weighing six pounds, fifteen ounces. She has blonde hair and hazel eyes and is perfect."

Jack and Marion were sitting in the living room holding hands. They were ecstatic and shed tears of joy. "A girl!" said Marion.

"Yes, a girl. The mother has a seven-day stay in the hospital, and she can spend as much time with the baby as she wants. She has ten days to decide to finalize the adoption."

"So anytime during these next ten days the mother can change her mind and decide to keep her baby?" asked Marion.

"Yes," replied Father Mac, "she can. But I will keep you informed daily of her decision. I wouldn't worry about that too much though. The mother was engaged to be married to the father, but they called off their wedding. She has chosen to place her baby for adoption. Our attorney in Mitchell has drawn up the adoption papers, so when the mother is ready, she can sign them."

"Has she seen or held her baby yet?" asked Jack.

"No," replied Father Mac. "She chose not to. Sometimes it's easier for the mother that way."

Father Mac continued, "On June 10, you would drive to Mitchell to sign the adoption paperwork and fill out the birth certificate at the hospital. You would need to decide on a name for your daughter."

"That sounds nice—*your daughter*," said Jack.

"After all the paperwork is done, you get to bring your daughter home!"

"And you said that we can name her whatever name we want?" asked Jack. "We get a new birth certificate?"

"Yes, you can name her whatever you want!" replied Father Mac. "We just need to get past the ten-day required waiting period."

Jack and Marion were excited yet apprehensive hearing this news. They knew that the next ten days would be difficult to get through, knowing the mother could change her mind, and if that happened, they wouldn't get the chance to meet the baby girl after all. Father Mac assured them that he would give daily updates, and he would pray for them every day.

He did call every day, and the report was always the same. "The mother is doing very well, and she has told the nurses that it would be best that she not see or hold the baby as it would tear her heart out."

"Oh, that poor woman. I can't imagine what she's going through. My heart goes out to her. I pray that she finds happiness and that she marries someday and has a family," said Marion.

June 6 was the discharge date for the mother from the hospital. Father Mac called with the news. "Today the mother signed the adoption papers and has gone home. It was a difficult thing for her to do. She wanted her baby girl to have two parents. She has opted for a closed adoption. I guess you know that this means no contact, which is what you wanted. She wants to get on with her life and have a new start."

Jack and Marion felt deep gratitude to her for making this huge sacrifice, thinking only of the baby girl and not of herself. They felt relieved. It would be wonderful to get a good night's sleep for a change. They both made a vow that they would be the parents she was hoping for. They were starting to feel excited, but they still had four days to go. They felt guilty for being so excited and happy when the birth mother was going through the hardest time of her life.

Father Mac called again the next day, "I wish you could go get your baby today, but we do have to wait those ten days. In the meantime, you could gather some baby things together to bring with you when you come to get your daughter."

Marion said, "I can't hear that enough—*your daughter*. It sounds wonderful." She was beaming.

The attorney called the couple to set up a time to meet at the hospital on June 10. "The birth mother has already signed," he said. "You will have a birth certificate to fill out, so you will need to decide on a name for your daughter. Be sure to bring a baby blanket, diapers, and whatever else you will need for her. The hospital will give you a care package, so if you're missing anything, it might be in there. Then let's meet at the hospital at 10:30 a.m."

Jack and Marion were beside themselves. The baby girl was *their* daughter! They made it through those ten days. They wanted to shout out from the rooftops their wonderful news but decided to wait until they had the baby in their arms. Jack and Marion spent the whole week getting the house ready for their new baby. Marion cleaned out one cupboard to make room for bottles and formula. She moved a spare dresser into the baby's nursery for her diapers and clothes. She painted the walls a pretty light green color and decorated them with happy pictures from nursery rhymes. They had borrowed a crib from a family member earlier and were also given some diapers, pins, bottles, and a baby blanket. Marion put a pretty sheet on the mattress and placed stuffed toys around the edge.

The new parents were so excited and happy that they didn't get much sleep the night before they were to pick up their daughter. They packed the car with a blanket, diapers, diaper pins (this was before Pampers), baby powder, and bottles in the morning. The attorney would meet them at the hospital at ten thirty in the morning for signatures and to fill out the new birth certificate. The name they picked out for their daughter was Susan Jane Steckelberg. The first name, Susan, means lily. Lilies are feminine and represent the promise of a pure and fruitful life. The middle name, Jane, means "gift from God" or "God is gracious." Jane is also a much-used name in the Steckelberg family.

In the morning, very nervously, Jack and Marion dressed up in their Sunday finest to meet their new daughter Susan. This was a special day. The car packed, they arrived at the hospital a little early, very nervous and ecstatic at the same time. Both shaking, they went inside and took the elevator to the maternity ward. The nurse at the desk asked if they were there to visit someone. Jack replied, "Yes, we are meeting our attorney to sign adoption papers, then to take our daughter home."

"Oh yes, you're the Steckelbergs!" said the nurse. "I will be the one to get your baby girl ready to go. Congratulations to you both! She is a good baby. Come with me and I'll show you your new daughter."

They came to a large window with some baby bassinets, a few holding babies. The nurse pointed out the one in the front. "This one is your new daughter. Isn't she a sweetheart?"

Jack and Marion lovingly gazed at their new baby, tears rolling down their faces. Jack said, his voice cracking, "She's beautiful."

Marion said, "Oh, she's beautiful. I can't wait to hold her!"

The nurse said, "Very soon. Follow me to the meeting room, and you and your attorney can go through the adoption paperwork. While you're doing that, I'll get your daughter ready. We have a gift for you too!"

Jack and Marion sat down at the table, nervously waiting for the attorney. He arrived shortly thereafter and said, "What a great day this is! I love days like this when I can witness such a happy occasion!" Following the introductions, he went on to explain each of the forms they were to sign. The birth mother's part of the paperwork had been signed four days earlier. Since the birth mother chose a closed adoption, several of the lines, such as name and address of the birth mother, were covered up with black strips of paper. The name the birth mother chose for her baby was for ten days only, and that was also covered up with a black strip of paper. This ensured there would be no contact with the baby or with the adoptive family. The birth mother did not want to be found. Being single, she could not provide a father for her baby, as it was next to impossible for a single woman to raise a child on her own in the 1950s. There were no government programs to help financially at that time, so a very small percentage of mothers were able to keep their babies.

The information the attorney had was that the mother wanted her baby to be placed in a Catholic home. He added that their new daughter was of Dutch descent, and if she ever wanted to open the adoption records, she could do so when she turned eighteen. (This last thing turned out to be untrue.) With that, the birth certificate was filled out with Jack and Marion listed as the parents. (This would be the *second* birth certificate, as the birth mother also filled out a birth certificate in a different name, which was known only to her. I wouldn't know for many years that there were two birth certificates with entirely different names.)

The attorney decided to stay to witness them meeting their daughter for the first time. He didn't want to miss this joyous occasion. The nurse returned with a big bag full of gifts from the hospital that was given to all the new mothers. It was filled with a blanket, a dress, bottles, diapers, and diaper pins—everything needed for a new baby, even bibs, booties, and rattles. When Jack and Marion laid their eyes on those things, they knew this was really happening. Their daughter would wear that dress and lay on that blanket. The nurse handed it to Marion and said, "Congratulations, Mom and Dad!" Jack and Marion both got teary-eyed. But the best gift was coming next.

The nurse came in carrying their new baby girl. She carefully transferred the baby to Marion's arms and said quietly, "Here's Susan, your new daughter."

Marion melted. She said, sobbing, "Hi Susan, I'm your new mommy."

Marion then carefully transferred their daughter to Jack. He was quiet, just gazing at his new daughter. "And I'm your daddy," he said. "Our prayers have been answered. We are now a family." And with that, everyone in the room was in tears.

This is the story of my journey through life
To find my biological mother
Even though we weren't searching for each other.

It was a closed adoption.
All records were sealed, never to be opened.
We were never meant to find each other.

"For this child I prayed, and the Lord has granted me my petition."
—1 Samuel 1:27

10

Sue

I made my appearance on May 31, 1955, at 8:20 in the morning at St. Joseph's Hospital in Mitchell, South Dakota, weighing six pounds, fifteen ounces.

My hair was blonde, my eyes were hazel, and I was a healthy baby. I spent the first ten days of my life at St. Joseph's Hospital. During that time, I never met my mother, and I didn't know my name. The nurses were so nice; they took great care of me, feeding and rocking me. But there was one special lady who spent some time with me on one of those days, and I imagined her holding me and talking to me, even singing to me. I was wrapped in a blanket, which she took off to count my fingers and toes. She wasn't one of the nurses. I don't know what she said, but I got the feeling that she knew me. I was with her for most of that morning. She was crying.

Before saying goodbye, she fed me a bottle of formula for lunch. She picked me up and held me to her shoulder, patting and rubbing my back. Still crying, she said goodbye, handed me back to the nurse, and started to leave. As she got to the doorway, she turned around and said, "I love you. Have a happy life."

1955 Happenings

- Gallon of gas: 23 cents
- Average new home price: $10,950
- Average yearly wages: $4,130
- Average hourly rate: $1.00
- Average new car price: $1,900
- President: Dwight D. Eisenhower
- Kentucky Fried Chicken is introduced.
- Crest is introduced.
- McDonald's opens.
- Disneyland opens.
- The microwave oven is invented.
- Seat belts are installed in new cars.
- TV dinners are introduced.
- Rock 'n' roll music gains in popularity.
- Polio vaccine is declared safe and effective.
- Rosa Parks is arrested.

I had imagined that I would have been introduced to a lot of family members by now, and passed around from person to person, each one holding me and talking to me. But so far, I'd only seen this one lady. I knew she wasn't my mother, but she was pretty special.

I was then whisked back to my place in the nursery. I wanted to be held by that lady again. All the other babies around me were going home. I was the last one left and was beginning to wonder if anybody was coming to take me home.

Years later, Phyllis would relay this story to me about her mother spending some time with me at the hospital. She never asked her mother what she said to me, and her mother never told her. I wish I could have met her. Knowing how close this family was, I realize that saying goodbye to me that day was one of the hardest things she'd ever had to do.

Finally, after ten days in the nursery, my mommy and daddy, Jack and Marion Steckelberg of Pukwana, South Dakota, came to get me. My new mom and dad signed all the adoption papers, which were then sealed and filed at the courthouse in Mitchell.

My dad was tall, clean shaven, handsome, and so loveable. His skin was dark brown from working outside. I felt so safe in his arms while he held me. He had such a nice soothing voice that I loved to hear him talk. He smelled great too.

He was born and raised on a farm north of Chamberlain, South Dakota. Chamberlain rests along Interstate 90, eight miles west of Pukwana. Chamberlain is along the Lewis and Clark Trail and borders the Lower Brule Lakota Sioux Indian Reservation. It is home to Al's Oasis, a tourist attraction and rest stop—where coffee is still five cents!—and Dignity, a fifty-foot-tall sculpture of a Native American woman, honoring the Lakota and Dakota cultures. Dignity overlooks the Missouri River at the rest area outside of Chamberlain.

My mom was a pretty petite Irish lady with red hair and a kind face. Her smile was so warm, it melted my heart. Her voice was soft and tender, and I loved her immediately. Finally, I got my Forever Family, and I was happy. I was looking forward to leaving the hospital. The nurses there were nice and all, but it wasn't my home. I would get to see my new home soon.

My new home was our farm north of Pukwana, a small farming community along Interstate 90, in the east central part of the state. The town's name is a Native American Ojibwa word meaning "smoke of the pipe of the Great Spirit." Pukwana was a small town, but it had the necessities—post office, hardware store, general store, gas station, grain elevator, church, saloon, two cemeteries, and a school for kindergarten through twelfth grade. The town was famous for its turkey races, which brought people in from miles around.

We arrived at the farm late in the afternoon. The driveway was very long, and the house was orange. Three steps led to the entryway, where a water pump stood by a sink. This was where we washed dishes since there were no faucets. Through the next door was the kitchen, a large living room was straight ahead, then to the right were two bedrooms and a closet in between the bedrooms. One of the two bedrooms was my room—the nursery, which held a crib, a dresser, and a rocking chair. Off the living room to the left was a door that led to a screened-in porch.

Outside was the entrance to the underground storm cellar. The door was very heavy and covered the entrance. Several steps led down to a one-room shelter with a dirt floor, which housed two chairs and a shelving unit. We made use of that shelter many times to be safe from the storms. In the fall, Mom used it to store her canned fruits and vegetables, since its temperature was cool and perfect for food storage. Most farmhouses did not have bathrooms but did have an outhouse, which was the case for ours. It was a small shack built over a hole in the ground and served as our bathroom. Thankfully, I did not have to use that, as I had my own little potty chair, but my parents did.

Out at our farm one day, my Steckelberg grandparents asked how the Catholic Charities adoptions work. Dad explained, "We applied through the Sioux Falls diocese, which covers several towns from Sioux Falls to Chamberlain, and the priests all work together to match up adoptive parents and babies. We were lucky that we could adopt in less than a year's time."

"Did you get any information about the birth mother? Do you know her nationality?" asked my grandmother.

"We were told Susan's nationality is Dutch, but we didn't get much information about the birth mother, other than she was unmarried and couldn't provide for her baby," said Dad.

"We're so happy for you and your family," said my grandfather while holding me and smiling at me.

Friends and family were so happy for Jack and Marion that

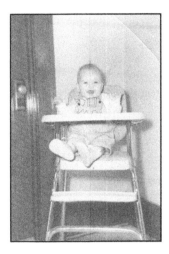

they held baby showers for me, which I got to attend. My mom received everything she was going to need for me, so much that the gifts covered the entire living room. There were bibs, rattles, cloth diapers, diaper pins, a stroller, a crib mobile, bottles, baby lotion and powder, and lots of pink and yellow outfits.

"Oh, Marion, your new little one is so sweet. I'm so happy for you and Jack!" exclaimed one friend. "Could I hold her?"

"Sure," said Marion. She took me over to the lady. I was passed around to several of the ladies at the shower, then laid in a bassinet.

"How long did it take to adopt?" asked another.

"It was less than a year from start to finish, which surprised me. I thought it would be a longer wait than that," replied Marion.

"You were meant to have her. It was God's will," said another. Everyone agreed.

Our family attended St. Anthony's Catholic Church in Pukwana, a cute little white church with a tall steeple and a church bell, which rang every Sunday morning announcing mass to the townspeople. It was at the end of Main Street, all four blocks of it. The first Sunday after my arrival at the farm, I was baptized in the Catholic faith by Father Mac. The Sacrament of Baptism is an act of faith and obedience to the commands of Christ.

Baptism declares that I am a follower of Jesus Christ. It is a public confession of my commitment to Jesus and is an important foundation for Catholic and Christian life. Baptism is a symbol of Christ's burial and resurrection. A water baptism signifies burial of my old life and resurrection from the dead. It's a symbol of my new life as a Christian. Goodbye to the old life; hello to the new life. This fulfilled my biological mother's stipulation that I go to a Catholic family.

Adoption: A beautiful way to build a family.

11

Sue

M om and Dad were getting the hang of being parents, and in 1958 they decided to try to adopt a second child so I could have a brother or sister. They contacted our priest again and filled out the paperwork to get the process started but found they did not qualify due to the age cutoff of forty. They were saddened about that news and realized instantly that I would be an only child. Coming from families with siblings, they knew the importance of having brothers and sisters. Siblings grow up together, they know each other's strengths and weaknesses, they have someone other than a parent to ask advice of, and they stick up for each other. They would have liked for me to have a sibling, but that was out of the question now. But they were thankful to have me and were determined to give me a great home as an only child.

Mom and Dad taught me very early on that I was adopted. The word *adoption* means "loved twice." The first is by the birth mother placing her baby for adoption so her child can have a wonderful life. The second is by the adoptive parents loving their new daughter whom they chose. They read a book to me called *The Chosen Baby* by Valentina P. Wasson over and over again, starting from the time they brought me home from the hospital:

> Once upon a time in a large city there lived Mr. and Mrs. Brown. They had been married for many years. They had been as happy as could be and were still young, and only one thing was wrong. They had no babies of their own, although they always longed for a baby to share their home.

I always knew they chose me to be their daughter. I understood what adoption was, at least as far as my young mind was capable of understanding.

I thought about the question of adoption as a child, and though it wasn't painful, it gave me a lot to ponder. What is the definition of a "real" mom? Is she the one who gave me life? Is she the one who adopted me? First and foremost, an adoptive mom has to have the desire to be a mother. A real mom can tell if her child is sad or happy, not by seeing, but by feeling. She has to be soft, yet firm. She has to give up her freedom and dedicate herself to this addition to the family, as well as to her husband. She has to make decisions to benefit the three of them. She has to be willing to make sacrifices in time and money, not to mention cooking and cleaning. And last, but not least, she has to have thick skin to handle the tough times. It's not only who you're born to or have shared DNA with that makes a family. Adoption goes much deeper than that.

My birth mother gave me life, but it was my mom and dad who nurtured me. They got up at three o'clock in the morning to give me a bottle and rock me to sleep when I didn't feel well. It was they who comforted me after a terrible nightmare.

They read me a story every night before bed. They loved me unconditionally and called me their daughter. They chose me! They were my real parents.

I had lots of cousins around who visited our farm occasionally. When they would leave to go home, I would wish that I had a brother or sister to play with. But since I was an only child, my cousins were my playmates, and I was satisfied with that.

Our farm had pigs, cows, geese, lambs, and chickens. Farm living was exciting. I fed the lambs with a bottle, and my pet goose, Goosie Gander, liked to strut around the yard with her babies. Mom and I gathered the eggs every day, planted a garden in the spring, and canned the fruits and vegetables at harvest time. Dad was the boss of his own farm. He plowed the fields to plant corn and wheat and took care of the cattle and sheep. He loved to hunt and fish whenever he got the

chance. Pheasants and grouse were plentiful at our meals, as well as just about every kind of fish, especially catfish, my favorite.

I loved my childhood. I was interested in what was going on around me, and I felt safe. Every day after school, I turned on our black-and-white television set and watched my favorite children's show called *Captain Eleven*, which aired from Sioux Falls, South Dakota. Captain Eleven's uniform was something like a spacesuit, but without a helmet. The show aired with this introduction:

> Captain E-leven, today's man!
>
> One man in each century has been given the power to control time.
>
> The man chosen to receive this power has been carefully selected.
>
> He must be kind. He must be fair. He MUST. BE. BRAVE.
>
> You have fulfilled these requirements and we, in the outer galaxy, designate to you the wisdom of Solomon and the strength of Atlas.
>
> YOU . . . ARE . . . CAPTAIN . . . E-LEVEN!

In 1960, Captain Eleven came to Pukwana to do his show. In my eyes, he was at the top of the list of famous people. This man was bigger than life to me. He appeared in front of the Powers' Dry Goods Store on Main Street with the town's kids gathered all around. I was walking with my dad, and the closer we got, the harder I was squeezing his hand like my life depended on it. Captain Eleven saw me and said, "Come on up, honey!" Well, I dropped my dad's hand so fast and ran up to Captain Eleven. He picked me up and held me throughout the show. That was my first brush with greatness. *Captain Eleven* was popular all over South Dakota, and in a house in Mitchell, sixty miles east, some other kids would also be watching the show on their black-and-white television set throughout the coming years. Little did I know then that these kids in Mitchell were my half-siblings.

I was adopted into the very old and storied Steckelberg family from Germany. The name *Steckelberg* means "steep hill." A branch of the family governed over one area of the country and lived in a castle called the Steckelberg, but it is in ruins now. The remains of a once beautiful rose garden rest at the base of the hill among the statuary, and the outline of a moat is still visible. Decades later, I visited this castle and placed my hands on those ancient walls. I felt the Steckelberg family connection and heard those voices whispering from the past.

My Steckelberg grandparents played a big part in my life, as most of our holidays were spent on their farm. My grandpa was a tall, large, muscular man, whose handshake was like a vise grip. It was painful. He had dark weathered skin from working outside on the farm north of Chamberlain and in his enormous garden for so many years. Grandma was a petite lady, not even five feet tall. She was very sweet, but also tough. I felt like I was a part of this family right from the start and knew no different. Even though I was told I was Dutch and not German, I *felt* German. I felt the connection, even though the bloodline wasn't there. I adored my grandparents and loved spending time with them. I never once thought that I wasn't a part of this family. (Decades later, I would find out that I really *am* part German after all!)

Grandpa bought the old homestead after his father's death. This was the house he grew up in. He lovingly built a front porch addition onto the original house. I felt like this was my house too, and I was always welcome there. It was a part of my family's history.

On Christmas Day, their house was packed with no fewer than twenty relatives getting together for food and fun. It was a ritual every year to cut down a Christmas tree from the woods behind the house. Those old, beautiful bubble lights were strung all around the tree, a dish of ribbon candy on a table.

Every year, Grandma hung up a curtain in the living room and handed us grandkids a stick to be used as a fishing pole. It had a string tied to it and a clothespin at the end of the string. Grandma was on one side of the curtain and us kids on the other side. We took turns "fishing," tossing the fishing pole over the curtain, Grandma attaching something onto the clothespin, then tugging. We caught a fish! On the line was a gift for that particular grandchild. We loved getting our presents that way. Before we left for home, she had one more surprise for us: a gift from her hatbox. It was round and deep, with a lid on top and strings dangling down the side with the grandkids' names on the end of the string. We all gathered around Grandma; she lifted the lid off the box and held it up while we found our name and lifted out another small gift, usually a candy cane. My cousins and I celebrated Christmases together for many years. They always treated me like I was one of their own, never an outcast.

Fishing was a big part of our lives. We lived on the catfish from the Missouri River. Dad grew up fishing with his dad and brothers, and whenever they went fishing, catfish was supper that night. He taught me how to fish early on by filling a bucket with water, putting a catfish in it, and giving me a stick with a string and hook on it and a stool to sit on. I al-

ready knew I was a Steckelberg through and through, but if I needed any confirmation, this fishing lesson cemented that. I was "hooked" on fishing from then on.

Grandma was a champ at cooking catfish; she could make it crunchy on both sides, the meat white, tender, and flaky, and the backbone peeled right off. No bones bitten into, ever. After my fishing lesson, I got to go with Dad to do some "real" fishing. Mom cooked the fish we brought home, and it was just as good as Grandma's.

Dad was also a hunter and went pheasant hunting every year. Mom cooked a mean pheasant! With Dad doing the hunting and fishing, we would never go hungry. He brought home grouse, pheasants, deer, fish, rabbits, and even a moose once.

Whenever we joined Grandpa and Grandma for a meal, Grandpa said grace in German. "Komm, Herr Jesus, sei unser Gast. Und segne, was Du uns bescherret hast." (Come, Lord Jesus, be our guest. And bless what you have bestowed on us.)

It was beautiful. He had learned the native tongue from his father and grandfather.

He sang this German love song many times:

Du, du liegst mi rim Herzen (You Are in My Heart)

Du, du liegst mir im Herzen, Du, du liegst mir im Sinn,

Du, du machst mir viel Schmerzen, weisst nicht wie gut ich dir bin.

Ja, ja, ja, ja, weisst nicht wie gut ich dir bin.

(You, you are in my heart, You, you are in my mind.

You, you cause me much pain. You don't know how good I am for you.

Yes, yes, yes, yes, you don't know how good I am for you.)

So, so wie ich dich liebe, So, so liebe auch mich.

Die, die zartlichsten Triebe, Fuhl ich allein nur fur dich.

Ja, ja, ja, ja, fuhl ich allein nur fur dich.

(So, so as I love you, So, so love me too.

The most tender desires, I alone feel only for you.

Yes, yes, yes, yes, I alone feel only for you.)

Doch, doch darf ich dir trauen, Dir, dir mit leichtern Sinn?

Du, du kannst auf mich bauen, weisst ja wie gut ich dir bin!

Ja, ja, ja, ja, weisst ja wie gut ich dir bin!

(But, but may I trust you, You, you with a light heart?

You, you know you can rely on me, You do know how good I am for you!

Yes, yes, yes, yes, you do know how good I am for you!)

I always loved hearing Grandpa Steckelberg sing this love song because he was singing it to Grandma. I felt so connected to the Steckelberg family every time I heard him sing it. I felt I was German myself. The fact that I was adopted was never forgotten, just set aside. It was something I didn't think about very much.

I heard on a television show once that an adopted child was told by a family member that he was *in* the family, but not *of* the family. Thank God I never had to hear that. I even think that if Mom ever heard anyone say that, she would have given them a lecture on adoption. I've always felt that I was a part of the Steckelberg family.

Going to Grandpa and Grandma Steckelberg's was always an adventure. Gathering the eggs, climbing up the corn bins, and playing in the old, abandoned vehicles kept me entertained. I traveled the world in those beat-up cars. Feral cats were everywhere, and when Grandma brought out the slop bucket full of grease, it was comical to see the cats running from every direction for that treat. They ran into each other in their frenzy as they wanted to be the first to get to this tasty treat. Since the cats were wild, they didn't like to be around people, and they weren't very friendly. Their kittens were sweet though.

Mom's mother, Margaret Brady Moore, died of diphtheria when Mom was twenty-one so I never knew her. She was one of the Brady girls whose parents settled in the area and were originally from Ireland. Mom's father, Joseph Moore, moved to Seattle after Margaret's death to work for the Boeing Company building airplanes. During his many years out there, he traveled back a few times for visits with family. He loved spending time out at our farm. Upon retirement, he moved into the Old Soldiers' Home in Hot Springs, on the western side of South Dakota. His parents were also from Ireland. My Grandpa and Grandma Moore could imagine what it was like to be transplants. Their stories always fascinated me because I felt like I was a part of them.

It's not the DNA that is responsible for the parent-child bond;
It is love and total commitment.

12

Sue

Farm life is a good life for a kid. I never gave much thought about being adopted or being an only child. Life was good. I would have loved to have had a brother or a sister, but I didn't, and it was all right with me. I was a part of a very special family whom I loved, and they loved me.

Sundays were spent at our pretty little Catholic church in Pukwana. During the Easter season of 1962, my Catechism class completed the requirements for First Communion. We started with the Sacrament of Reconciliation, which taught us to confess our sins to a priest. Every Catholic church has confessionals somewhere inside, and every Saturday, they are open for a certain amount of time. The priest is in the middle, with another confessional on each side of him. There is a lightbulb at the top of each one that is on if someone is inside. I went into one, shut the door behind me, and knelt on the kneeler inside. This cued the light. The priest opened a small door inside and said, "Bless you. In the name of the Father and of the Son and of the Holy Spirit, Amen." We both made the sign of the cross.

I said, "Bless me, Father, for I have sinned. It has been [number of days, weeks, months, or years] since my last confession." Then I confessed my sins. He gave me penance and told me to say three Hail Marys. I said, "I am sorry for my sins."

He said, "I absolve you of your sins. Go in peace, in the name of the Father and of the Son and of the Holy Spirit. Amen." We would make the sign of the cross again. I exited the confessional and knelt at a pew. Whatever the penance was, I would say the prayers. Penance was done.

After that, we learned about the Sacrament of the Eucharist. Since everyone takes the Eucharist together, it is called Communion. It is done toward the end of every mass. Starting at the front of the church, everyone taking Communion would get up row by row and stand in line in front of the priest. When it was my turn, he said, "Body and Blood of Christ."

I answered, "Amen."

The host represented the Body and Blood of Christ. It was a small, round, flat piece of bread that would be placed on my tongue to be dissolved and swallowed. I opened my mouth and stuck out my tongue, then went back to my place in the pew for the end of mass. I felt renewed and "kissed by God." We sang a song to celebrate our togetherness again.

I spent eight glorious years on our family farm. But farming is a way of life that is dependent on the weather. If crops get flooded out, frozen, dried up, or eaten by grasshoppers, there is no money to be made. Dad, after fifteen years on the farm, decided that farming wasn't profitable anymore. He was hired by the federal Department of Agriculture at the Morrell meatpacking plant in Huron, South Dakota, supervising the kill floor for the cattle and hogs. A plus was that this was a Monday-to-Friday job, not at all like farming, which is twenty-four hours a day, seven days a week. Dad would experience the life of hogs and cattle from beginning to end. He had seen and taken part in the circle of life for these animals, first at the farm with their births, then to complete the circle at the meatpacking plant with the end of their life.

We held a farm auction that summer of 1963, then packed up the rest of our belongings in the pickup and headed for Huron, South Dakota.

Goodbye, Pukwana; hello, Huron!

Huron is in Beadle County in east central South Dakota, just fifty miles north of Mitchell and the seventh largest city in the state. Incorporated in 1880, Huron is home to the South Dakota State Fair and the World's Largest Pheasant, which is a huge pheasant statue on top of a building.

Mom and Dad had gone to Huron the previous month to find a house and to get to know the town while I stayed behind with my aunt and uncle. I looked at this move as an exciting adventure, yet I was a little nervous and scared. What would it be like living in a town? I'd only known farm living. Would I miss gathering the eggs every day? Would I miss the animals? What would it be like to have neighbors just a few feet away instead of miles? Would I have friends? Mom and Dad asked these same questions. They had never lived in town either.

We moved into a cute little white house. There were lots of kids in the neighborhood, and I needn't have worried about making friends, because by the end of the summer, I'd made friends with them all. My parents were getting used to town living, and Dad was enjoying his job at the meatpacking plant.

One of my friends lived across the street in a really big house, and she had eight brothers and sisters. Somehow, the subject of me being adopted came up, and she asked, "What's it like being adopted?"

That was the first time I'd been asked that question. I replied, "It's just like everybody else. You have a mom and dad, and I have a mom and dad. The only difference is that we're not blood related. But they're all I've ever known. My biological mom wasn't married, and she couldn't keep me. She had to give me away."

My friend was quiet for a bit, then said, "You mean they're not your real mom and dad?"

That question stung, and more than just a little bit. How dare she ask that! How rude. I was so much a part of the Steckelberg family that I sometimes forgot I was adopted. I replied, "They *are* my real mom and dad! They raised me, and they're all I've ever known. I almost got a brother, but at that time, they were too old to adopt another child."

"Gosh," said my friend, "I have five brothers. Maybe you

could have one of them!" She was serious, and I can see why—they had a houseful!

A month or so after our arrival to Huron, we had gotten settled into our house and Dad was learning his new job. There was a knock at the door one summer morning, and a lady was standing at the front door all dressed up and holding a big basket full of different things. She said she was from an organization called Welcome Wagon. We had never heard of it. The nice lady explained that she was there to welcome us to the community and to give us gifts from several businesses, along with lots of coupons for meals, housewares, and other things. She informed us about the downtown businesses and where all the stores were located. It was like Christmas! In the bag were several kitchen utensils with business names on them. We made very good use of all of those gifts and coupons. What a nice welcome to Huron!

Something she encouraged us to do was to start accumulating S&H Green Stamps. Started by the Sperry and Hutchison Company, these stamps were given to customers for their purchases at various businesses. The businesses giving out the green stamps were the most popular ones and the busiest. The customers would receive a set number of stamps for every dollar they spent, and the stamps could be redeemed for items in the Sperry and Hutchison Company catalog. S&H Green Stamp stores were open in many towns where folks could redeem stamps and pick up more booklets.

About sixty miles south, in a house in the city of Mitchell, the lady of the house also received a visit from Welcome Wagon and had a kitchen drawer full of those S&H Green

Stamp booklets. Having gone through the Great Depression and the World War II years, she knew all about stamps and saving money. With a houseful of children and a husband, she had to make her money stretch as far as it could go. The green stamp store, on a corner in downtown Mitchell, was where she could redeem her stamps for needed household items. Just about all of her kitchen appliances were acquired with the stamps. This lady was Phyllis, although I didn't know her yet.

Our neighborhood was full of kids, and there was so much to do. We played softball often through three seasons—spring, summer, and fall. All we had to do was show up, and we'd get added on to a team. I loved these games, but every now and then, I would have to leave early because of a migraine headache. The only relief I could get from those was to go to bed in a dark room with a cold washcloth on my forehead. For an active kid, this was a horrible thing to have happen in the middle of a good softball game. There was no medication available for those headaches at that time.

Our Steckelberg family had several generations of violinists, and Dad wanted me to be among that next generation. My dog, Queenie, didn't like that idea at all. She ran lickety-split for the basement when she saw me get my violin out because the screeching hurt her ears.

During junior high school, I was still playing the violin, but I was getting a lot better, so much so that the Huron Symphony Orchestra selected me for a spot in the second violin section. Granted, it was the very last chair, but I didn't care—it was the symphony. My favorite musical composition piece was "Rhapsody in Blue" by George Gershwin, written in 1924. We performed this piece for a few concerts, including one at the Bandshell, an outdoor stage with a "shell" around it in a park setting. Folks brought blankets and chairs, got comfortable, and enjoyed the music. We looked so professional, with the ladies in black gowns and the men in black suits with black bow ties. We played for the Firemen's Ball that same year, trading "Rhapsody in Blue" for waltzes. My parents attended, and I couldn't take my eyes off them, Mom in her pretty blue ball gown and Dad in his good black suit. They made good use of the dance floor that evening. I wished that night would never end.

In addition to practicing with the symphony all those nights, I still had Catechism to attend every Wednesday evening. My schedule was full. I got a big surprise when I found out that my priest from Pukwana, Father Mac, would be my Confirmation teacher. He decided to join us in Huron for a couple of years. The Sacrament of Confirmation affirms the growth process that as the human body grows, our soul also needs to grow and strengthen for the years ahead. It also means that I accept responsibility for my faith and my continued growth throughout my life. My parents had guided me thus far, and now it was up to me to continue that growth. I knew my biological mother wanted me to be raised in a Catholic home, and she would be very happy to know that I was.

I needed to pick the name of a saint for my Confirmation name. That was easy. It would be Theresa, my favorite name of all. I discovered that Saint Theresa is the patron saint of headache sufferers. This is fitting because I suffered from migraine headaches. So did Saint Theresa, and I felt that bond with her instantly. I wondered often if my biological mother or family suffered with those awful headaches.

All of these life experiences were orchestrated especially for me, with God guiding me on this path to meeting my birth mother. I can't go wrong by putting my trust in my spiritual guidance, which is God. He is always leading me, guiding me, and giving me support when needed. The hard part is learning to tune in to and decipher those messages.

"And whoever welcomes one such child in my name welcomes me."
—Matthew 18:5

13

Phyllis

Phyllis didn't know who had adopted her baby girl or where they lived, but she found herself looking at all the babies she saw in church. She felt good that her baby went to a Catholic couple, and she wondered if one of the couples in Holy Family had adopted her. She was comfortable with her decision and had no regrets. She eventually got her figure back by doing a lot of walking and sit-ups. She went back to roller-skating, going shopping with Delores, driving around with her friends, and going to movies and dances. Things were looking up. Dorothy was a constant presence in Phyllis's life, and they had lunch together often over at Dorothy's house, talking about the future and what was in store for Phyllis.

"I know that placing your baby for adoption and canceling your wedding is still pretty fresh, but do you have any ideas on what you want to do with your life in the coming years?" asked Dorothy. "Do you plan to stay working at the concrete company?"

"Yes, for now anyway. They've been so good to me, as you know," replied Phyllis.

"They sure have. You're lucky to have such a great boss."

"And who knows? Maybe I'll find a guy who will treat me like a queen someday!"

Dorothy was very happy to see that Phyllis was getting back to her old self, the one before Ed. She knew Phyllis made the right decision placing her baby for adoption. Dorothy felt like Phyllis was a lot happier, and she seemed to have a whole new outlook on life. She thought, *Phyllis is going to be just fine.*

That fall, Phyllis met Milt Brookbank, a US Army corporal who served his country in Korea. He was the ultimate Elvis impersonator. He worked as a car mechanic at the APCO station on Rowley Street in Mitchell. Milt succeeded in putting back the smile that had been missing from Phyllis's face for quite some time. They fell head over heels in love. He asked her to marry him that spring of 1956, and she said yes. They were married on April 18, 1956, at St. Mary's Episcopal Church, and Phyllis Cunningham became Phyllis Brookbank. The whole Cunningham clan came to the wedding, and everyone's faces were beaming, knowing what Phyllis had been through the previous year. The ones with the biggest smiles on their faces were Phyllis, Ethel, Dorothy, and Delores. This wedding was extra special as this was a new beginning for Phyllis. Out with the old and in with the new. It was time to shake off the past and look toward the future.

Phyllis wore a beautiful lavender lace wedding dress with a matching veil, and Milt wore black slacks and a white jacket. In later years, Phyllis's wedding dress made its way into their daughters' toy chest for playing dress-up.

Milt and Phyllis started their new life as a married couple, and Phyllis left her job at the concrete company. Milt's brother, Ivan, had been dating Phyllis's niece, Delores, and they married in 1958. Phyllis and Delores would now be sisters-in-law. The two girls started out as Cunninghams, and both were now Brookbanks. The two couples got together often, and Phyllis and Delores were tight.

Sadly, Phyllis's beloved dad, Thomas, passed away in July of 1959. His funeral was held at the Church of the Nazarene. He had been the family patriarch for the Cunningham family, and now Ethel would have to bear the title of matriarch. She moved in with Milt and Phyllis, as that is what families did during this time. There was no such thing as assisted living or retirement homes, so family members stepped up and helped their parents. Just two months later, Phyllis and Milt would welcome their firstborn, Michael. Phyllis was so happy to have her mom there with her.

This was how Phyllis had imagined her life all along. She was relieved of Ed, but she thought often of me, the baby girl she gave up. She often wondered where I was and what I was doing. And she remembered me and prayed for me every year on my birthday.

Their second child, Susan, was born in 1962. While Phyllis was in the hospital, her sister Dorothy came to see the new baby girl. Her visit was bittersweet as she also came to say goodbye to Phyllis. Dorothy and her family were moving away, and Phyllis was heartbroken once again.

Dorothy said, "Hi, Phyllis, where's your baby?"

Phyllis replied, "The nurse is bringing her in here in just a minute or two. Are you and hubby all packed and ready to go?" She and Dorothy had been through so much together. Dorothy was a big help for Phyllis when she was pregnant with me. She hated having to say goodbye, but she was in a much better position now with her husband and two children to keep her occupied, not to mention her mom living with the family.

"Yes, we're all packed and ready. I just wanted to stop here and see you first. I didn't want to leave without saying goodbye to you. I already stopped to say goodbye to Mom."

The nurse came in with baby Susan. She placed her in Dorothy's arms. "Oh, she's so beautiful! I so hate having to leave, just when you're starting your family." Dorothy made funny faces at Susan, who giggled.

Phyllis said, "I'll be all right, Dorothy. You helped me a lot in our younger years. And you saw me through my relationship with Ed and my pregnancy. I can never thank you enough."

"Oh, I'm so glad I could help you. I'll miss you so much." Dorothy started to cry, and so did Phyllis. Dorothy handed baby Susan back to Phyllis. "Goodbye, you two," she said, sobbing. Dorothy hugged Phyllis, and with that, she walked out of the room.

Milt and Phyllis's family kept growing, with Mary, born

in 1963, and then a year and two months later, Scott born in 1965. Milt continued working at the APCO station, and Phyllis managed the household. Ethel continued cooking for the family. They were happy and very busy.

In the fall of 1969, Phyllis drove to Huron for a funeral. Her friend Florence lived in Huron and had a daughter named Lee, who passed away at age fourteen. Phyllis attended the funeral at the Catholic church in Huron. She had often wondered where her baby girl went after she was adopted. Somehow, she got the idea that her firstborn went to Huron to live, and she wondered if her baby girl was a friend of Lee's or if they were classmates. They would be about the same age. She found herself scanning the church for teenage girls. She had the right idea, and unknown to Phyllis at this time, I not only lived in Huron but was a classmate of Lee's and was at her funeral.

And then more news. Phyllis's oldest brother, Clarence, passed away in 1971. Oh, why does there have to be so much sadness amid all the happiness? Phyllis was four months pregnant with their fifth child. So, last but certainly not least, five months after Clarence's passing, Debra made her appearance.

Milt and Phyllis raised their family in a three-bedroom, two-story house on South Montana Street in Mitchell. Ethel's grandchildren remembered her delicious meatloaf from their growing-up years. Supper was a sit-down affair with a "no hats at the table" rule. It was an active and lively household, and they were a close-knit family, just like it was when Phyllis was a child. With five children, something was always happening. Christmases were celebrated with gifts opened on Christmas Eve and stockings filled by Santa on Christmas morning around a beautiful, sparkling silver Christmas tree, loaded with ornaments, lights, and angels. The angels reminded Phyllis of her family members who had gone on before her. They gave her comfort.

The number five was a popular and significant number in this family, as Thomas and Ethel had five children, Milt and Phyllis had five children (although Phyllis would rediscover a sixth one many years down the road), and their daughter Debra had five children. And there would be yet another generation, Debra's son and daughter-in-law, who would also have five children. And the amount of time between Clarence's death and Debra's birth was five months. I also have some fives in my life. I was born in the fifth month, May, in 1955. Plus, I have five half-brothers and half-sisters. What can I say—I am a numbers geek!

"She is far more precious than jewels."
—Proverbs 31:10

14

Sue

Dad was offered a promotion at work that year, 1970, to federal meat inspector. We had a family meeting and discussed the details of the new job and whether he was going to accept the promotion. The downside was that we would have to relocate to Minot, North Dakota. After much discussion, we all agreed this would be a great opportunity for him. We'd be farther away from family but still within driving distance. So, at the end of my ninth-grade year, we moved once again, this time very far north. No pickup was needed on this trip; a big Allied Van Lines semitruck hauled all of our stuff to our new home. Minot or bust!

Minot is the fourth largest city in North Dakota, situated in the north central part of the state, approximately fifty miles from the Canadian border. It was founded in 1886 in Ward County. The Minot Air Force Base is located fifteen miles north.

Mom, a social butterfly, set about getting to know all the neighbors right away, and Dad started his new job as meat inspector. He traveled all around north central North Dakota stamping the meat packages with the USDA (United States

Department of Agriculture) stamp of approval. And the best thing about Minot—it's the home of the North Dakota State Fair.

In the fall of 1970 my parents enrolled me in the tenth grade at Bishop Ryan Senior High School, a Catholic school with priests and nuns as teachers and administrators. I rode the bus to school. The nuns wore the long black robes and habit, the tight part that goes around the face and head. Our homeroom teacher carried a ruler—but not for measuring. It was a strict school, and in my homeroom the boys were constantly talking and misbehaving, so our teacher would approach the offender at his desk and threaten to "box his ears." This involved a quick slap of the ruler against the offender's ear, plus a detention slip to boot. All this right away in the morning. It was always the boys who had no sense when it came to misbehaving around those nuns.

Our classes were the usual ones, English, math, and history. We also had a sex education class as part of our physical education program, but it was in its beginning stages since it hadn't been taught in the fifties or sixties. They taught about the male and female anatomy, what it means to be a virgin, and sexuality. It was weird and uncomfortable, and we just wanted to get it over with. Even the teacher had a red face.

Even though it was a strict school, I loved attending Ryan High. It did not have an orchestra, but I was secretly glad to be done with the constant violin practicing, and no one was happier than Queenie.

At the end of that school year, another classmate and I made plans for the summer. She was friends with kids from the public school, and this opened up a whole new horizon for me. The public school kids spoke a different language and dressed differently. It was 1971, and a lot of interesting things were happening around the world. Hip-hugger bell-bottom jeans were in fashion, along with midriff tops, platform shoes, and headbands. Hippies, peace, love, and flowers were all around, and I wanted all of it! Hello REO Speedwagon, Black Oak Arkansas, and Grand Funk Railroad.

My straight hair was very long, almost to my waist, and throughout the dishwater blonde color, I had streaks of brighter blonde put in. This was painful. It cost seven dollars for this three-hour ordeal at the beauty college. The student brought out what looked like a swimming cap with about a hundred tiny holes all over it. She stretched that over my head and took a little crochet hook and started pulling strands of hair through every one of those tiny holes. Ouch. The worst was over. I was glad about that, but I still had to sit there with that cap on for roughly an hour while she put the color goop all over those strands and let it sit for a while. Then it was time to rinse and take the cap off. I enjoyed that hairstyle for quite a while but decided not to go back for an encore. Once was enough. I often wondered if my birth mother or her family had that horrible straight hair. I would find out many years later that my birth mother was very fussy about her hair also and had it fixed once a week, come rain or shine. The things we girls do to look good!

I met Jim that summer. He was a handsome, worldly, charismatic guy, about five feet, ten inches tall, and easy to carry on a conversation with. He had long hair, but most of the guys did during that time. And was he ever cute. We had everything in common. We spent a lot of time together that summer. I was a dreamy-eyed sixteen-year-old, and I fell for him hard. I just knew that he was the one for me.

My first job was at Sears at the mall. I sold hot dogs, a bag of chips, and pop for twenty-nine cents at a stand outside the main entrance to the mall. It was a busy stand. I loved the freedom this job allowed me as I was only sixteen and they trusted me enough to run the stand all by myself. The best part was spending time with Jim after work, and he would give me a ride home!

My parents didn't quite know what to make of this new me. I was talking funny, saying things like "groovy," "far out," and "can you dig it?" They wanted their old Sue back. On top of it all, I was dating a guy with long hair. They didn't understand why a guy would want long hair.

The first time Jim picked me up at home in his car, he honked the horn for me. I had started for the door when my dad said, "You sit down. Jim can come to the door like a gentleman when he picks you up." My dad commanded respect, and he wanted me to be treated with respect as well. After that, Jim always came to the door to pick me up, and this made my dad very happy.

My parents again enrolled me in Ryan High School that fall for my junior year, but I didn't want to attend Ryan anymore. The public school was where I wanted to go because all my new friends went there. My parents said no. They were hoping that the structured environment of the Catholic school and having all my girlfriends from the tenth grade there would make me want to stay.

"But Mom, I really like the people at the public school, and I fit in. Please let me go to school there!" I begged.

"I know you want to go to the public school, but your dad and I feel that Ryan High School would be the best for you," replied Mom. "You're already enrolled for the junior year, so the case is closed for now. We'll talk about it again before your senior year starts."

Their decision was made. I was going back to Ryan High, and that was final. I did go back to Ryan—for one week. On Friday, I put all my books in my locker, went home, and told my parents I wasn't going back. I was so stubborn—my poor parents, having to deal with that terrible teenage attitude.

I won that battle and got to attend the public school after all. It was different from Ryan High, not a nun or priest in sight. My classes were enjoyable, and Jim and I got to eat lunch together every day. Everything was going well, and my parents had warmed up to Jim and even started liking him. They still didn't understand why he wore his hair long, but I loved it! He was so handsome with that long hair. We even got to where we wore matching headbands.

By then, Jim and I were ocean deep in love. We often talked about our future together. I dreamed about living happily ever after in a cute little house with a white picket fence. These were the hopes and dreams of my sixteen-year-old self.

Then the bottom dropped out in March. I passed out in church one Sunday morning. Mom and I went to the car. She asked me if I thought I might be pregnant. I wondered why she would ask that; she must have known something. I said, "I don't know."

Mom made an appointment for me to see a doctor and to get a pregnancy test the next day. I was nervous. My doctor was a male, which I wasn't thrilled with at all. Unfortunately, there were none of those nifty sticks invented yet that a girl could pee on and have a "pregnant" or "not pregnant" answer shortly. So, here I am, sixteen years old, getting ready for the test.

"Undress and put on this sheet," said the doctor. "I'll be back in a minute."

He came back in and rolled a stool to the end of the table. "Scooch down to the end of the table and put your feet in these stirrups, please," said the doctor. He inserted something metal and cold. All I could do was pray that this would end soon. Those stirrups were cold and hard on my feet. I felt completely humiliated and wanted it over with now.

The test was positive. I got a good scolding from the doctor. His face was red with anger. "Susan, you are only sixteen, and you are incompetent to be a mother and raise a baby. I am ordering you to place this baby for adoption. You have no business keeping this baby."

I was surprised at his being so mad. Maybe there *were* a lot more girls in this same situation as me. But it made me angry and embarrassed for him to talk to me that way. He had no right to do that. Unknown to me, sixteen years earlier, my birth mother went through this very same scenario.

The doctor talked to my mom after he left the exam room. After that, it was a long, silent drive back home. All Mom said was, "I'll give your dad the news when he gets home from work."

I went directly to my room until supper, which was quiet. Dad didn't say anything at all. My parents were disappointed in me but would be very supportive in the long term. They just needed some time to get over the shock that I was pregnant at sixteen. The year was 1972. Pregnant teenage girls could not attend public school. All that work to get to the public school was for naught. I had to drop out.

My mom found a place in Minot that had just opened and catered to unwed pregnant girls. Evidently, there were a lot more girls in the same situation. I was starting to realize why the doctor was so angry with me. The place was called the Oppen Home for Unwed Mothers. Mrs. Oppen had had a dream of opening a home for unwed mothers similar to the Crittenton homes of the fifties, only she wanted hers to be more like a comfortable home, not an institution. Upon her death, her will allowed for the money to buy the land and build the home. Her dream was realized.

The home was very nice and cozy. It was carpeted with beautiful furnishings and pretty pastel colors on the walls. There were five bedrooms, four for the girls and one for the director. The girls' rooms had two twin beds covered with brightly colored comforters, two dressers, two desks, and two closets. They were like college dorm rooms. The kitchen was huge and had all the latest appliances, complete with two ovens and an industrial-sized refrigerator. We had a wonderful cook the year I was there, and the meals were delicious. The home could house up to eight girls, and an additional eight girls could come for the daytime classes. The classes were not the typical math, English, or social studies but rather sewing, cooking, baby care, and nutrition.

Some girls opted to place their babies for adoption, so they didn't have to attend the baby care class. The first class had just two live-in girls and four daytime girls, of which I was one. We each had a job to do at lunchtime and were taught to set the table properly, with cloth napkins, a water glass, and several pieces of cutlery. Even though we were all pregnant and unwed, the staff treated us like we were young ladies and respectable citizens.

The rules were pretty lenient, not at all like the Crittenton homes. The girls who lived at the Oppen Home could come and go as they pleased. They could go to movies or go shopping with their families and friends, and they didn't have to put on a wedding band, like the homes of the fifties. They could have contact with the father of their baby but not at the home. Their evenings and weekends were free. They could get to know the other girls and be friends with them. I myself made friends with two of the girls who came to the daytime classes.

"Our public high school has night classes available," Dad said to me one day. "They are three nights a week, two hours each night. Why don't we attend those classes together? We can both get our high school diplomas that way." He hadn't graduated high school because he wasn't allowed to play football after he turned eighteen, which was the school rule then. He got mad and dropped out of school altogether.

"I like that idea! Let's do it!" I said. We enrolled in the

classes we needed to complete high school. Dad needed one year of classes, and I needed two years' worth. It was a win-win for us both. Dad and I spent some quality time together, and we talked on the way to and from school. Our relationship grew stronger.

I attended the Oppen Home in the day, then went home for supper and on to the public school with Dad. Sometimes we'd stop at home after and pick up Mom and go out for ice cream.

Dad finished his classes and earned his high school diploma in 1972, just thirty-six years late. He called his mom and gave her the news that he had graduated high school. She replied, "Well, it's about time!" I graduated from the Oppen Home and was part of the first class to do so. The home would go on to have full capacity for many years after. Years later, I found out that my birth mother had the option of living at one of these homes for unwed mothers, but she chose not to go there. For me, it was a wonderful place, and I'm so glad that Mom found it for me.

Jim and I were together a lot during this time, and when I felt like it was time to go to the hospital, I called him to come and get me. I was in labor for eighteen hours, and he was there with me the whole time. We didn't know if the baby would be a boy or a girl because there were no tests available at that time to determine the sex. A nurse came into my room and asked, "Will you be keeping your baby or placing it for adoption?"

I replied, "Keeping," while gritting my teeth during a contraction pain.

We welcomed our baby boy, Bradley John, to the world in December of 1972. Jim and I were both just seventeen years old. All of the teachers and the girls from the Oppen Home came to the hospital to see me and my new little son. Jim, of course, was a daily visitor at the hospital and at home.

I had completed one year of high school with Dad, so instead of night classes, the high school had a new day program for students like me in one room of the school. I could go there anytime during the day, pick up assignments, and either work on them there or take them home. I could even take Bradley with me. A teacher was on duty all day to answer any questions. I earned my high school diploma in August of 1973, just three months later than the rest of my class.

After graduation, I got hired at the Ward County Auditor's Office in the courthouse. My job was to record financial expenditures and payments in the big heavy ledgers that were kept on steel shelving in the back room. I liked my job very much—the pay was great, and so were the benefits. And working in the beautiful Ward County Courthouse was icing on the cake. Bradley and I moved into a two-bedroom apartment in a nice part of town just a few blocks from my parents' house. I enjoyed life and kept busy with Bradley and my job, and my parents loved being so close to their grandson!

"I have loved you with an everlasting love."
—Jeremiah 31:3

15

Phyllis

After Debra was born in 1971, Phyllis went to work at Herter's in Mitchell. It manufactured and sold its own line of hunting, fishing, and camping gear. Phyllis's job was selling guns and sporting goods. She loved working there and stayed until it closed in 1978.

The year 1978 was a rough one for Phyllis as her second oldest brother, Harvey, passed away in May and her mother, Ethel, in October, five months apart. (There's that number five again.) Phyllis was heartbroken once again. Ethel and Phyllis loved each other and had lived through so much together, and now the house would seem so empty without her. Ethel's funeral was held at the Church of the Nazarene in Mitchell, and life in the Brookbank household carried on without its family matriarch.

Phyllis started working at Woolworth's in 1979. This would be her favorite place of employment by far and would always hold a special place in her heart. Woolworth's was a department store and sold items for every area of the house, from kitchenware and curtains to automotive accessories, parakeets (yes, parakeets!), and anything else a person might need—or *not* need.

Phyllis worked in every department of the store, but she enjoyed the toy department the most. When the new toys were delivered for the Christmas layout, she couldn't wait to open those boxes. Her boss scheduled her at the checkout often because she knew how to count back the change, thanks to her math classes in school, as the registers at that time didn't tell the change amount due to the customer.

During Corn Palace Week in the fall, Woolworth's set up a big table in front of the store and sold caramel apples. Phyllis would sit at the table and dunk the apples in the caramel that was in a very large pot at the end of the table. She became known as the "Caramel Apple Lady." People would come from miles around to attend the festival and take home some of those famous caramel apples, the caramel "a secret recipe." (And, once again unknown to Phyllis, this was the *second* time that she and I would cross paths.)

Milt bought and ran his own service station, called Milt's Service, specializing in radiators. In addition to her work at Woolworth's, Phyllis was the bookkeeper, and their children helped Milt whenever they could. All of the kids worked there at one time or another, and they learned the ropes of working on cars and of customer service. The station was a busy one.

Phyllis and Milt's kids all grew up during the 1980s, which was all big hair and parachute pants. Each one had the big hair, but Debra wins the trophy in that category. She had not just "big" hair, but "big, teased, and sprayed" hair, and every strand had to be in place before she presented herself to the public, minus an entire can of Aqua Net hairspray!

One by one, the first three—Michael, Susan, and Mary—married and had children of their own, making Milt and Phyllis grandparents. The new grandparents bought the house next door and sold their old house to Michael since he and wife Kathy had no desire to move away. Susan and Mary both opted to move to Virginia, which meant goodbyes and lots of tears. The years were filled with weddings, funerals, dinners, Christmases, and lots of vacations with friends and family. Phyllis was sad to see Susan and Mary leave but very happy to have Michael and Kathy next door and Scott and Debra still at home. She wouldn't be lonely, as she still had her family, Delores, many friends, and her church to keep her busy.

"Adoption is a journey of faith, from beginning to end."
—Johnny Carr

16

Sue

My parents always told me that I could open up my adoption records after I turned eighteen, even offering to help me with it. During the summer of 1974, Bradley and I went on a road trip to the Black Hills of South Dakota with a detour to Mitchell. This was our first road trip together, and we'd been looking at pictures and planning the trip for months. Shortly after my nineteenth birthday, we left Minot in our trusty old brown Rambler and headed for Mitchell.

One stop I wanted to make was to the courthouse in Mitchell to find out what I needed to do to open my adoption records, mostly out of curiosity. It wasn't a necessity that I find my birth mother; I mainly just wondered if I had any brothers or sisters. I asked my parents if they would be all right with that. They told me once again that they were behind me 100 percent and to let them know if they could help in any way. I know that they prayed for Bradley and me when we left to go on that trip, and Mom lit a candle at our church. She prayed for us to have a safe trip and to find the answers I was looking for. She also prayed that I wouldn't forget them if I did find my birth family. I could never do that.

At the courthouse in Mitchell, I was very nervous when we walked into the clerk of courts office. A lady approached the counter and asked, "May I help you?"

I said, "Yes, I'm interested in obtaining a court order to open my adoption records that are filed here. I was born at St. Joseph's Hospital here in Mitchell on May 31, 1955, and adopted on June 10, 1955."

She asked, "What is your name?"

I replied, "Susan Jane Steckelberg."

She excused herself and said she'd be right back. When she came back to the counter, she said, "There are no records under the name Steckelberg. Your biological mother probably named you. Do you know that name?"

That surprised me. I wasn't aware that there would be a different name or that she could have named me at all. I had no idea what it could be.

I said, "No, I didn't know the records would be under a different name. All of the names and addresses were covered up at the time of signing."

The clerk shook her head and looked sympathetic. "Yes, the birth mother fills out a birth certificate before leaving the hospital. I have to know that name in order to find the records."

I was dumbfounded and speechless.

She continued, "I'm so sorry, but when the information is covered up like that, it means it's a closed adoption and the records are sealed." She placed her hand over mine and said quietly and gently, "Your biological mother evidently doesn't want to be found. I wish I could help you, but there's nothing I can do. I'm so sorry."

"Your biological mother doesn't want to be found." That sucker punch came out of nowhere. I felt like I had just slammed into a brick wall. All those years earlier, my parents' attorney gave them the wrong information. Those adoption records were never meant to be opened, ever. This realization hit me hard. I thanked the lady for checking on it, and Bradley and I walked out of the office. I felt like a zombie. I was stunned. There was a bench out in the hallway that I almost fell into. I sat down hard, staring into space. All these years I had been hoping to find my biological mother someday and now I realize that it's impossible. I did a lot of thinking about my situation that day on that bench.

I thought, *Now what? Now what do I do?* I looked over at Bradley; he was tracing the designs in the marble floor with his finger, and I felt better instantly. He was my whole life. I would find out who my biological parents and siblings were when I was dead, and that was okay with me. Besides, there was not one thing I could do about it, so I might as well accept it.

I said to Bradley, "Let's go see Mount Rushmore!" When we left the courthouse, I closed that door for good in more ways than one. In that one hour's time, I felt like I had become a different person leaving the courthouse than the one who came in. I felt stunned, but I decided to never think about it again. And I didn't. I shut that door for good.

Jim and I were together for six years. As the years wore on, it became clear that neither of us was ready for marriage, so eventually the day came when we broke up. A few weeks after our breakup, a couple of my friends dragged me out to a bar one weekend to cheer me up and enjoy the evening. There I met David. I wasn't ready for a new relationship, and my conscience was saying, *Don't get into a new relationship this soon*, but I wasn't listening. I didn't know it at the time, but it was a rebound relationship.

David worked for the Kmart Corporation, training as an automotive department manager. Five months down the road, David was offered his own store in Worthington, Minnesota. He asked me to marry him, I said yes, and we quickly married. The moving van came, our things were loaded up, and we headed for Worthington. We got into a set schedule with his hours at the store and my hours at the animal clinic where I was employed. Bradley started kindergarten. Then came another promotion for David in the spring of 1978, only eight months later, to manage the automotive department in a brand-spanking-new store in Mitchell, South Dakota, which he accepted. I declared, "Hey, this is neat—I was born in Mitchell!"

Mitchell: Home of the World's Only Corn Palace! Bradley started school at Whittier Grade School, and I got a job at Verschoor Motors checking in the new cars. David helped open up the new store and commenced managing the very busy automotive department.

By the end of 1978, our marriage ended and David requested and received a transfer to Washington State to another Kmart. He moved on, and Bradley and I stayed in Mitchell. We moved into a two-bedroom apartment in a townhouse complex on the edge of town by the junior high school. We had neighbors on both sides, but it was quiet and was more like a house than an apartment.

By that time, my parents had moved from Minot back to Chamberlain, and we were now just sixty miles apart. Dad retired after a heart attack that led to open-heart surgery, so following his recovery, they moved back home, much to my delight.

Bradley (or Brad, as I was calling him) and I started back to church at Holy Family Catholic Church, and he was baptized. Wednesdays were for Catechism, and he learned about and made his First Communion.

I left Verschoor Motors, and after a Christmas season at JCPenney, I was hired on full time at the Commercial Trust and Savings Bank in the proof department, encoding checks and deposit slips. Three years later, I was promoted to the bookkeeping department to maintain the children's Kelly Club savings accounts. The accounts were a great way for children to save money, and the program's mascot was a big green frog. Since I was the custodian for these accounts, I was appointed "Kelly the Frog." The costume consisted of a green one-piece suit and a giant papier-mâché frog head. The Kelly kids benefited by attending a free movie or free roller-skating party once a year. The movies were held at the Logan Theater, and the theater owner and Kelly the Frog would get up on stage and have yelling contests to see which side could yell "Kelly!" the loudest. That being over—thank goodness—Kelly would head upstairs to watch the movie from a nice, quiet room. When the movie was over, Kelly held the door open for the kids and waved, "Goodbye, until next time!"

The roller-skating party at the skating rink for the Kelly Club kids was fun, but the frog head didn't fit that well, and it was virtually impossible to try to skate and hold the head on at the same time. I was hanging onto the railing for dear life, going around the rink with one hand while holding onto the frog head with the other, and all the while, the kids were whizzing past me on the floor. I felt like I was a ninety-year-old frog on her last legs.

During my years at Commercial Bank, the president sent me to Woolworth's to get caramel apples as a treat for everyone at the bank. Every fall during Corn Palace Week, Main Street

was covered with rides, food trucks, games, and the always present caramel apple table in front of Woolworth's, with the best caramel apples around. The lady who waited on me had a nametag that said "Phyllis," but I dubbed her the "Caramel Apple Lady." She was a sweet lady, was very personable, and had the nicest smile. Her hair was short, blonde, and always perfect. I would say, "I'd like a dozen caramel apples for the bank employees, please. The president is treating us!"

She would reply, "Well, that's really nice of him! Coming right up!" And she would proceed to dunk twelve apples in the big vat of caramel. Unknown to me at the time, the "Caramel Apple Lady" was Phyllis, and this would be the second time we would cross paths.

Since the Kelly Club accounts were so successful, I was given another savings account to maintain, called Instant Money Plan, or IMP for short, the mascot being an "imp," or leprechaun. I had on green tights, a green blazer with a belt, and the typical green leprechaun hat. I did a television commercial for that one and talked about the benefits of the Instant Money Plan with writing appearing on a screen next to me. Sure wish I could have seen that finished commercial.

That commercial was shown on television all over Mitchell and was probably seen in the Brookbank household.

"Adoption is another word for love."
—Nancy McGuire Roche

17

Sue

My dad had been battling cancer for all of 1983 and was admitted to the veterans hospital in Sioux Falls, South Dakota, several times. He was eventually transferred to the VA hospital in Minneapolis. Mom called early Christmas morning with the news that Dad had just passed away. On Christmas Day. My wonderful dad was gone.

His funeral was at the Catholic church in Chamberlain. Dad's death hit me hard. I couldn't believe he was gone. He loved me for who I was and accepted me even with all my flaws. He was my rock and my protector. He gave me the best things in life—his time, his care, and his love. I drew the lucky straw when it came time to hand out parents. He spent countless evenings working with me on my multiplication and division tables with flash cards he made himself. My dad was never serious, always joking, and he was funny. I think I got my sense of humor from him. I always carry the memories of us going to night school together in my heart. He taught me respect for others and for my country. He will be a part of my life, heart, and soul forever. I was so thankful and blessed to call him My Dad.

I didn't handle his death well. Not thinking straight, I made the poor decision to leave my wonderful job at the bank that spring.

Our Mitchell Vocational Technical College offered courses in accounting so I opted for the Secretarial/Accounting program that fall of 1984. This would give me a couple of career choices. I learned shorthand and put those skills to work in the school office.

Following graduation, there were no secretarial jobs available, so I went to work at Kmart. It was meant to be short term, but the job was so enjoyable that I stayed. I worked in the sporting goods department during pheasant hunting season, when hunters from all over the United States came for their hunting licenses. The line of hunters would stretch from the rear of the store, out the front doors, and into the parking lot.

Mom would drive over from Chamberlain occasionally to visit and to attend the musicals that Brad was in every year of junior and senior high school. She would come to celebrate our birthdays with Brad and me, and we would go to Chamberlain for her birthday and for Christmas and Thanksgiving. She loved coming to Mitchell because she loved shopping at all the stores, especially the clothing stores.

In 1987, Brad and I were still attending Holy Family Church but were invited by friends to attend the Mitchell First Church of the Nazarene. The music at the Nazarene church was much livelier and the sermons by Pastor Koker were so interesting that Brad and I would attend the Catholic church on Sunday morning and the Nazarene church on Sunday evening. This went on for many weeks because it was hard for us to leave the Catholic church. The Church had been my rock and my foundation throughout my entire life, and it was a very difficult thing to leave; Holy Family Church played a big part in both my life and Brad's life. Brad and I eventually did become members of the Nazarene church and left Holy Family. "The Church of the Nazarene bonds together individuals who have made Jesus Christ Lord of their lives, and sharing in Christian fellowship."

My first Sunday morning there, I saw the Caramel Apple Lady from Woolworth's in the pew behind me. She was sitting with her husband, Milt, and she told me she was the mother of Debra, a friend of Brad's in the youth group. Debra and Brad also attended the same junior high and high school, Debra a year older. She had been to our townhouse two or three times while in junior high school playing games on the Atari. I would later think back on those times and laugh at the fact that Brad's friend was actually his aunt.

This was the third time that my biological mother and I unknowingly crossed paths, and it continued since Brad and I joined the Nazarene church. Now, my birth mother and I were not only in the same town but in the same church as well.

18

Sue

DOUG ELLWEIN

Brad's high school English teacher was Doug Ellwein, who had taught there for thirty-four years and knew most of the families around town. He had seen many of Mitchell's youth come into his class and graduate from high school. College was the choice for some, military for others, and going out into the work force and/or marriage for the rest of them. He enjoyed teaching those kids. They came out knowing the difference between *there, they're,* and *their*. He still remembers the names of most of them and keeps in touch with quite a few also. He pays attention to the choices they have made after high school. He knows who went to which college and who got married or moved away or both.

Doug was well known around Mitchell, and everywhere he went, somebody knew him, or vice versa. What happened on this September day in 1988 at Kmart was just another chance meeting with one of his previous students, Susan Brookbank, or so he *thought*. He thought she had married and moved to Virginia, but evidently, he thought, they had moved back. He was anxious to hear about what she had been doing the past few years since graduation and when she started working at Kmart.

I was working my shift at Kmart in the sporting goods department that day. My uniform was black slacks, a blue shirt, and a red vest with a nametag that said "Sue." I had heard an announcement earlier for me to do a pickup at the service desk, so I headed on up.

I had to wait a bit as there was a gentleman being waited on there. He looked over at me as I was approaching the desk and said, very suddenly, "Hi, Susan!"

I turned my head quickly to see who was talking to me and said hello back. But I was thinking, *Who is this guy? Do I know him from somewhere? How does he know me?* I was puzzled.

"When did you move back here?" he asked.

"I've lived here for a few years now," I replied, still puzzled.

"Didn't you live out east?" he asked as the service desk clerk refunded his money.

"No. Worthington, Minnesota, is as far east as I've been," I said, even more puzzled.

"Didn't you live in Virginia?"

"No, I've never been there!" I replied, as I reached over the counter to pick up what I had gone up there for.

"Aren't you Susan Brookbank?" he asked.

"No, I'm not," I said, wondering, *What the heck?*

"Really! You look just like her," he replied.

I shrugged.

He kept on. "Are you related to the Brookbanks?"

"Not that I know of," I said, wondering how this man could

be so confused. I knew some of the Brookbanks from church, and Debra, of course. I shrugged again, shaking my head.

Doug does have a great memory for his students. He remembered Susan. He knew she lived in Virginia, at least he *thought* she did. He thought I looked exactly like her. But that wasn't the end of it, not after that perplexing conversation. This was Doug's first brush with the Susan Brookbank lookalike, and he needed to get to the bottom of this. He knew that I just *had* to be a sister or a relative, and he was going to find out which one it was. He made it his mission to talk to Susan's mother, Phyllis, about this, and Susan's sister, Debra, who just happened to be in his English class. He couldn't wait until the next day when he would see Debra and she could give him an answer to who this Susan who works at Kmart is.

The next day, after English class was done, he drilled Debra for answers. Is your sister Susan working at Kmart? Do you have *any* sister working at Kmart? Is she a relative? Do you know who she is? She looks just like Susan! Debra just kept saying "I don't know! I don't know!" over and over again.

Doug didn't get very much information from Debra, so he decided to try Phyllis. He was trying to figure out how to approach her. He was going to call her on the phone, but while eating at Fanny Horner's Restaurant with his family that weekend, in walked Phyllis. He was thinking, *This is my chance to talk to her.* So, he marched right over to her table and asked her point blank if she had a daughter working at Kmart.

He said, "Phyllis, I'm Doug Ellwein, Debra's English teacher. I have a strange question for you. I was wondering if your daughter Susan is back from Virginia and working at Kmart?"

Phyllis replied, a bit apprehensive and uncertain where this was going, "No, she's still living in Virginia."

Doug continued, "Well there's a young lady named Susan working at Kmart, and she looks exactly like your Susan. Are you sure she's still in Virginia?"

"Yes, she's still there! I don't know who this person at Kmart is," said Phyllis, thinking, *What the heck, does he think I don't know where my own daughter is living?*

Doug replied, "She just *has* to be related to you somehow." He had no idea just how related I was.

Doug was persistent and determined to find out who I really was. He kept track of this story and still asked Debra from time to time at school if she knew who I was yet. Of course, the answer was no every time. Debra wasn't at all curious or concerned about the situation. At the time, the only way she was interested in knowing me was as Brad's mom.

I still had no clue or suspicion. So strong was my belief that I was of Dutch ancestry and from a Dutch settlement somewhere in South Dakota that I didn't once entertain the thought, *Gee, I wonder if this Brookbank family could be my biological family.* I gave it no thought. Besides, with my adoption records sealed tight, there was no way I was ever going to be able to find my birth parents anyway.

Doug liked to tell stories in his classes, usually about some funny accident that he had, but soon he would have another story to tell. Doug didn't know how close he was to solving this mystery.

19

Sue

Following that conversation with Doug at Kmart, I was thinking that Susan Brookbank might be Phyllis and Milt's daughter. I knew they had several children, and I guessed that Susan was one of them. Phyllis and Milt always sat behind me in church, and we sat in the same place every week. We would visit a little before and after church services, then they'd pick up Debra and I'd pick up Brad from the youth service and we'd go our separate ways. The next time I saw them at church, I was going to ask about Susan.

I was anxiously awaiting their arrival at church that Sunday. When they finally arrived, I greeted them and asked, "Phyllis, you have a daughter named Susan, right?"

Phyllis replied, "Yes, she is our oldest daughter, why do you ask?"

"Well, I had a very strange conversation at work this week," I said. I repeated the conversation that I had with this fellow who I later discovered was Doug Ellwein. I told her that I didn't know him, other than him being the English teacher at the high school and that he sure thought that I was their daughter Susan. "Do you think I look like your Susan?"

Phyllis looked at my face for about a minute, then said, "No, I don't think so."

I replied, "I guess it's just one of those things." And that was the end of that conversation. I thought nothing of it. After all, wouldn't a mother recognize the resemblance to her children better than a high school teacher?

A month later, the exact same conversation happened at Kmart again, only this time, it was with a math teacher. Again, she said I look exactly like Susan Brookbank. Once again, I couldn't wait until Sunday to tell Phyllis this story. I still had no clue about any of this.

Sunday came, Milt and Phyllis were in their usual places, and I took mine. After our usual greetings, Phyllis asked if anything interesting happened at work that week. I said, "Funny you should ask. This week a lady approached me in the toy department and introduced herself as the high school math teacher. It was the same darn conversation I had with Doug Ellwein. She thought I was your Susan."

Phyllis replied, "Well my week was interesting, because Doug Ellwein approached *me* at Fanny Horner's over the weekend. He asked me if I have a daughter working at Kmart! It's so strange because I don't think you two look anything alike!"

I had to see this for myself.

"I have four children. Two are adopted. I forget which two."
—Bob Constantine

20

Phyllis

Milt and Phyllis had been attending the Mitchell First Church of the Nazarene for several years and noticed that the parishioners tended to sit in the same place every Sunday. Milt and Phyllis were no exception, nor was the young lady who sat in front of the couple. Phyllis knew me as the mother of Brad, who was a friend of Debra's from high school. They knew I wasn't married, but that was about all they knew about me. Every Sunday, before and after the church service, we would visit and make small talk.

A curious thing happened at church the next Sunday. I greeted them with the usual "Hi! How was your week?"

Phyllis answered back, "Pretty uneventful, but good."

I then told Phyllis about the conversation I had with Doug Ellwein at Kmart that week. I told her that he thought I was her daughter Susan and that I supposedly looked exactly like her. Phyllis didn't think so though. But Doug had already approached Phyllis and asked her if she had a daughter working at Kmart. She started thinking, *Could it be? Could Sue be the baby girl I gave up for adoption in 1955?* She answered her own question immediately. *No! It's not possible! It's just a coin-*

*cidence. People look like other people all the time. Everyone has
a twin somewhere.* Phyllis needed to tell Delores about this.
After discussing it with her, Delores agreed that it was just a
coincidence.

The year was 1988. Phyllis was working at Woolworth's,
Milt was running his service station, and I was working at
Kmart. Scott decided to join his sisters Susan and Mary in
Virginia. Brad and Debra were in high school together, Debra
a year older. Phyllis and I by now were both involved with
church activities, Phyllis as a Sunday School teacher and me
as a helper. We visited on the phone occasionally about church
duties.

On one of our phone calls, after discussing church business, the subject of me looking like Susan came up once again.
I was still flabbergasted about that, and I blurted out, "This
is so strange. And what makes it even more strange is that
I'm adopted!" Now this is something I never talked about to
anyone, so why I would say this out of the blue is a mystery
to me. I suspected nothing. It never ever occurred to me that
this could be my biological family. After all, doesn't everybody
have a double somewhere? And besides, I had it in my head
that I was probably from around Corsica or another Dutch
settlement.

"I'm adopted," she thought. *Wheee,* Phyllis was a mess. Her
head was swimming, and she needed to get Delores in on this,
as Delores and her husband also attended the First Church
of the Nazarene. "Delores! What do I do?" Phyllis exclaimed.
"You and I have got to talk! I can't handle this. Could Sue be

the baby girl I gave up for adoption in 1955? Delores, I have to find out her birth date!"

Delores and Phyllis had talked about me often throughout the years, wondering where I was, what I was doing, and what I looked like. Delores thought Phyllis should invite me over for lunch and ask questions, but not too many questions. She didn't want it to look suspicious. Phyllis liked that idea, so she invited me to lunch. We became friends and learned we shared numerous similarities, the biggest one our love for all things Wizard of Oz, since each of us had a dedicated room for Oz memorabilia. That same year, the children's theater produced the play *The Wizard of Oz*. We each knew someone in the play, so we went to it together.

Phyllis found out my birth date in the May 1988 church newsletter, where the May birthdays were listed by date, but without the year. So, now Phyllis knew my birthday was May 31. All she needed was the year, but by now, Phyllis was pretty sure I was the biological daughter she had placed for adoption. I looked like Susan, I was born on May 31, and I was adopted. Phyllis just needed to find out where I was born and what year. She thought maybe she'd call me and just come right out and ask how old I was, but she felt she had to be sneaky about it. She had to have a cover story and a reason for calling. She was worried. She never thought she'd find herself in this situation. The adoption records were sealed. She had seen to that. She didn't know what to do. She was curious now and decided to keep going with her plan to get my birth date. Phyllis didn't want to ask me straight out what my birth date was as she wasn't prepared to answer questions I might have, such as, "Why do you want to know that?"

She figured out what the story would be (though neither of us could remember what it was years later) and just worked in the question, "And how old are you going to be on your birthday?" real innocent. She was thinking, *If she says thirty-three, I will faint. I don't know if I'm ready to hear her answer, but it's out there now, so no backing out. Okay, Phyllis, you can do this.* She braced herself.

I replied, "Thirty-three."

And there it was. It was a good thing Phyllis was sitting down because she would have fallen over in a dead faint otherwise. She counted thirty-three years back—to 1955. Phyllis was 99 percent sure now that I was her daughter.

Phyllis called Delores immediately after. "Delores! I just talked to Sue on the phone, and I asked her how old she is going to be on her birthday. She said thirty-three, which means she was born in 1955. I'm almost 100 percent sure she's my daughter who I placed for adoption!"

"I agree! I think we've found her!" exclaimed Delores.

Every Sunday after that, unknown to me, Phyllis and Delores compared me to Phyllis's other kids and watched my every move in church. They stared at me while I sang in the choir. They checked my profile, how I stood, how I looked when talking or singing. Most of the time, they thought I looked like Scott. Sometimes Susan, sometimes Debra. I had no idea they were doing that.

During the year 1989, Phyllis and Delores, having known the truth for a few months, were unable to face the hardest part: telling me. Phyllis was so afraid that I would take the news badly and be angry. She picked up the phone at least a hundred times only to chicken out and hang up. Besides, she realized that calling me on the phone wasn't the way to give me this news. It had to be in person. She and Delores were the only two who knew the secret, and Phyllis couldn't tell anybody else. She was positively bursting.

Phyllis asked me over for lunch one day. She thought she'd tell me then. Lunch came and went, and she chickened out again. She just couldn't stand the thought of me being upset, storming out the door, and wanting nothing to do with her. Delores asked, "Would you like me to come along with you?"

Phyllis replied, "No, I need to do this myself."

Delores agreed. "I think you're right, but if you change your mind, give me a call."

It was nearing the end of 1989, and I was engaged to be married to Bruce, the manager of I-90 Truck Haven in Mitchell. He and his two sons, Justin, who was in the fourth grade, and Jeremy, who was in the third grade, had just moved to Mitchell from Sioux Falls the previous year. Bruce had accepted a promotion to manage the truck stop in Mitchell. He and his sons had been attending the Nazarene church for a few weeks, and I met Bruce through our singles group. Most of our dates were spent at the I-90 Restaurant, enjoying delicious apple pie with ice cream, being served by Debra, Phyllis's daughter. (I still had no clue about any relation to the Brookbanks.)

The calendar changed from 1989 to 1990.

1990 Happenings

- Gallon of gas: $1.34 per gallon
- Average new home price: $123,000
- Average yearly wages: $28,960
- President: George H. W. Bush
- *The Simpsons* airs for the first time.
- Popular toys: Nintendo Game Boy, Holly Hobbie
- Microsoft releases Windows 3.0.
- Demolition of the Berlin Wall occurs.
- East and West Germany reunite.
- Smoking is banned on cross-country flights in the US.
- J. K. Rowling begins writing *Harry Potter and the Philosopher's Stone.*
- Exxon Valdez oil spill happens.
- Universal Studios Orlando opens.
- Popular movies: *Home Alone, Dances with Wolves, Pretty Woman, Die Hard 2*
- Popular musicians: Jon Bon Jovi, Janet Jackson, Garth Brooks, Billy Joel, Aerosmith, Cher, Red Hot Chili Peppers, Whitney Houston
- Best Motion Picture: *Driving Miss Daisy*

Our wedding would be held on January 20, 1990, at one o'clock in the afternoon. Our wonderful Pastor Lothenore would be the officiant. The church congregation was invited, and Phyllis was very excited to be a part of my and Bruce's big day. She planned in advance the dress she was going to wear that day. She was so excited, and she looked forward to meeting both of our families, but she was mostly looking forward to meeting my mom. She couldn't let on to them who she was, though. Not yet anyway. On our wedding day, Phyllis and Delores walked in and chose a place to sit. Delores was on the aisle and whispered to Phyllis, "Why don't you switch places with me, that way you can see your daughter better." Pastor Lothenore married Bruce and me in the Mitchell First Church of the Nazarene, and we became an instant family of five: Bruce, me, Brad, Justin, and Jeremy. Phyllis enjoyed that day very much. She visited with Bruce's parents, my mom, and our families, although she was bursting at the seams with the knowledge she was carrying.

On their way back home after the wedding reception, Phyllis and Delores discussed some more ideas about how to inform me that I was Phyllis's biological daughter. "Delores, I just can't go another year without saying anything. This has *got* to be the year!" said Phyllis. She was determined to find a way.

Pastor Lothenore asked me if I'd be interested in taking the job as church secretary, and I accepted. My office was at the front of the church, and I had a big window where I could see the people coming in or going out the front door. The office was big, with lots of cabinets and a large L-shaped desk. I enjoyed my job working with Pastor Lothenore, and he was a great boss.

Phyllis would stop by to visit with me when she picked up her materials for Sunday School class every week. I still had no clue that Phyllis was anything other than the Caramel Apple Lady, and I never gave any thought to the comments made about me looking like her daughter Susan, other than that they were hilarious.

The season changed from summer to fall. Phyllis just finished another year of Crazy Daze sales at Woolworth's, where they were gearing up for the new layouts and for Corn Palace Week. At the church, I typed up the lessons for Vacation Bible School, which was ending shortly, and kept everyone in our church informed with the monthly newsletters. Bruce was getting ready for the yearly influx of bikers heading to the Sturgis Motorcycle Rally in August. We were all still getting used to each other, and the three boys were gearing up for the new school year.

The week of September 10, 1990, started out like any other. Pastor Lothenore had given his resignation the previous month, as he had been offered a church in his home state of Texas. He and his wife had just moved a few days prior. The church had a new pastor hired, but he wouldn't be there for another month, so guest pastors were serving during the interim. The church and the church office were abuzz with activity, the phone ringing constantly and parishioners coming and going. It was reaching a fever pitch; something was about to happen.

"Adoption is the hardest thing you will probably ever do in your life. You feel like your heart is being ripped out. But if you are doing it for all the right reasons, your life will be truly blessed forever."

—Laura Gladden

21

September 12, 1990

Phyllis stopped in to return a coffee pot on September 12, 1990. She had borrowed it for a ladies' function the week prior. By then, Phyllis and Delores had been keeping their secret for a year and a half, and Phyllis still hadn't found the courage to tell me.

That day, Phyllis peeked around the open doorway and said, "Hi, Sue! How's your day?"

I said, "It's a good one!"

"I'll be right back," said Phyllis, as she headed for the stairs going to the kitchen. She returned the coffee pot back where it belonged, then came back up the steps to my office. Phyllis came in and sat down in the chair in front of my desk. She asked, "How's everything going since Pastor Lothenore left?"

I replied, "Busy! It's crazy busy around here, and our new pastor isn't coming for four more weeks!"

Phyllis opened her purse and got out her checkbook. "I

need to renew my missionary magazine subscription," she said and started writing out a check.

I said to her, "You're not going to believe this, but somebody told me again this week that I look like your daughter Susan!"

I can't begin to describe the look Phyllis had on her face at that moment. She looked very, very serious all of a sudden. The color drained from her face, and she looked pale. She stopped writing and looked at me. She was quiet for a bit. I was beginning to worry. I didn't know what was happening. She sat back in her chair and thought, *Lord, I hear You. You're telling me that now is the time. All right.* Aloud, Phyllis said to me, "Sue, I have a story to tell you, and please don't interrupt me until I get this out." She looked up to the sky and prayed aloud, "Lord, be with me."

"Children are a gift from the Lord. They are a reward from Him."
—Psalms 127:3

22

September 12, 1990

Phyllis was leaning back in her chair and looking up at the ceiling. "I've been holding this in for a year and a half. I've picked up the phone at least a hundred times to call you, only to chicken out and hang up. I just ask that you don't interrupt me until I get the whole story out."

I knew that whatever she had to tell me was very serious. I didn't know what to make of it. I sat back in my chair and wondered, *What's happening here?* I was bracing myself for something, but for what? I didn't know. I only knew Phyllis from Woolworth's and from church, and we weren't *that* close, so what would she have to say to me that would be so serious? What the heck was this about? "Okay . . ." I said, scowling apprehensively. "I promise I won't interrupt." *What the heck?* She began her story.

Phyllis took a deep breath and said, "Okay, here goes." She began telling her story slowly, pausing between sentences. "On May 31, 1955, I gave birth to a baby girl at St. Joseph's Hospital here in Mitchell. She was born at 8:20 a.m. and weighed six pounds, fifteen ounces. I wasn't married, so I made the decision to place the baby for adoption so she could have a mother and a father. I specified that she be raised in a Catholic home as I was Catholic at that time. I never ever considered abortion. I wanted her to have two parents, which I couldn't provide, and wanted her to lead a happy and healthy life." She paused, looked at me, and said, "I think you are that baby girl."

Oh, dear Lord! I could feel the color drain out of my face. I said, "Are you serious?" I started to cry. I don't know if it was from shock or relief. This hit me hard, but in a good way. I was thoroughly floored. All I could say was, "Are you serious?" I collected myself enough to pause. My hands were covering my face. I looked at Phyllis and said quietly, shaking, "I was born on May 31, 1955, at St. Joseph's Hospital, and I'm adopted. I hope it's true."

Just a few clicks of the second hand on the clock was all the time it took to find the answer to years of questions.

Phyllis was instantly relieved to hear that. I could *see* the relief. She didn't know what my reaction would be. She thought maybe I'd be very angry, which was why it took her so long to say anything. So, hearing me say, "I hope it's true," she was finally able to relax. She had held that in for a long time.

All those years I had closed that door of finding my birth family and it hit me smack dab in my face in my church office. I finally understood what the conversation with Doug Ellwein was all about. And why people were mistaking me for her daughter Susan. I was sincere when I said, "I hope it's true," because I liked Phyllis. I had gotten to know her and Milt from Sunday church services, and I already knew Debra through Brad, and I thought they were pretty neat people. I thought if the rest of their family was as cool as those three, I was pretty lucky. I had known Phyllis for many years as the Caramel Apple Lady. Now I would know her as my birth mother.

If there's such a thing as a "good" sucker punch, this was it. I surely did not see that coming. Sixteen years ago, I tried to get a court order to open my adoption records, and sixteen years ago, I put it all behind me, never to think of it again. I had shut that door for good. Until this minute. And it was literally until this minute. I had no suspicions beforehand. I always thought I would be from one of the Dutch settlements around South Dakota. I asked Phyllis, my voice shaking, "Are you Dutch by chance?"

Phyllis replied, her voice shaking also, "No, no Dutch. Why do you ask?"

"My parents' attorney told them right from the start that I was Dutch."

"No, you're Scottish, English, and Irish. I wonder where he got the idea that you were Dutch!"

"Wow, I can't believe I'm not Dutch! Even more, I can't believe I'm Irish! My mom is Irish, and my dad and I used to always tease her every year on Saint Patrick's Day!" I said.

"I tried to open the adoption records when I was nineteen, but there was nothing under the name Steckelberg. They told me that I would never be able to open the records because it was a closed adoption and that we were never meant to find each other."

"Yes," Phyllis said, "that's right. I named you Kathryn Lynn Cunningham; that's why you couldn't open them. You didn't know that I named you. The papers are filed under that name. You also have a birth certificate with that name."

"Kathryn Lynn Cunningham," I said. "I like that name. It rolls off the tongue. It has a nice sound to it." I repeated, "Kathryn Lynn Cunningham. That was my name for the first ten days of my life!"

Phyllis got her small calendar out of her purse then, opened it up to the month of May and, shaking, showed me the name in the space for May 31—Kathryn Lynn. Phyllis said, "I've remembered your birthday every year since you were born." And with that, she crossed out Kathryn Lynn and wrote Sue Vrooman in its place.

Finding out she named me Kathryn Lynn was a surprise. No wonder I couldn't find out anything at the clerk's office in the courthouse. I asked, "Why Kathryn Lynn?"

Phyllis replied, "It's a name I have always loved. My son Michael's wife's name is Kathy, and Debra's middle name is Lynn, so I finally got my Kathryn Lynn! Oh, I have so much to tell you, and I don't know where to start! I can't believe I finally got this out. Oh, I can't stop shaking!"

Neither could I.

"I want you to know that I wanted to keep you, but I just couldn't. Your biological father and I never married. I felt that you deserved more than what I could give, which was a mother *and* a father." She continued, "You have two half-brothers and three half-sisters. Their names are Michael, the oldest; Susan, the one everyone was mixing you up with; Mary, the middle child; Scott; and Debra, who you already know."

"I always wanted a brother or a sister. Now I have five! I can't wait to see what they look like, although I already know Debra."

"I'm pretty confident that you are the baby girl who I placed for adoption, but what would you think of getting a court order to open the adoption records? Just to be sure? We both now know that the records are filed under the name Kathryn Lynn Cunningham."

"Yes, I think that we should definitely do that," I replied.

"Okay, I'll call the clerk of courts office and ask what we need to do to obtain a court order to open the adoption records or if we need to schedule an appointment with the judge," said Phyllis. I agreed. Shaking, Phyllis picked up the phone book, found the number, and called the clerk of courts office. She asked the lady on the line what the procedure was to get a court order to open adoption records. She told Phyllis that she would transfer her call to Judge Gerken.

"This is Judge Gerken. How may I help you?"

"Hello, Judge, my name is Phyllis Brookbank, and I live in Mitchell." She told him her story slowly. "On May 31, 1955, at St. Joseph's Hospital, I gave birth to a baby girl whom I immediately placed for adoption. I named her Kathryn Lynn Cunningham. It was a closed adoption, and the records are filed at the courthouse. I believe we have found each other on accident. I'm sitting at her desk at the Nazarene church right now. We are interested in opening the adoption records and would like to know what we need to do. Everything matches up. Her name is now Susan Vrooman, but she is known as Sue, maiden name Steckelberg. How do we go about applying for a court order to open the records?"

He repeated the information Phyllis had given him back to her to be sure that he had the correct information written down. Phyllis confirmed it. "Okay, first let's do this—Phyllis, talk to your family about it and make sure they're all right with opening the records. Talk it over with your husband, children, whoever you're closest to. And have Sue do the same thing. If she was adopted into a family and her parents are still alive, if she's married, if she has children, then she should discuss this with all of them, but especially her parents."

In a case like this, with a closed adoption, the judge wanted to cover every base possible. Uncovering an adoption can be unnerving as some family members might not take this news well. He wanted to make sure that everyone on both sides would be agreeable to opening the records. It can be a sensitive and delicate situation. The outcome isn't always positive.

Phyllis said, "Her father is deceased, but her mother is still alive and lives in Chamberlain. As of today, I now know their names—Jack and Marion Steckelberg. Sue also has a husband and children."

"Okay, I want you both to go home and discuss it with your families. Call me back tomorrow morning at eleven o'clock, and we'll see what needs to be done then. I can't stress it enough that I want to make sure that everyone is on board with opening those records."

"All right, Judge, thank you very much. We'll visit more tomorrow."

The thoughts going through my head were, *How am I going to break this news to Mom? It's going to be a shock for her, and she doesn't have Dad there to lean on. I have no idea what words to say to her.*

The call ended, and Phyllis looked at me, let out a sigh of relief, and said, "He wants us to discuss this with our families tonight, and if they give their blessings for us to get a court order for the records, Judge Gerken will help us with the next step. So, I'll talk to Milt tonight, and you talk with your mom and Bruce and Brad too. Then we'll meet back here tomorrow morning, and we'll call the judge again at eleven o'clock and he'll tell us what we need to do and where we go from there."

Neither of us made a move to get up to go. We were still in shock, but we were both grinning. I said, "Did you happen to notice that the phone didn't ring once during all this time, and nobody came in or out?"

Just then, the phone rang. I knew then that this was God given and that it was meant to be. It was still a shock, and even though it was a good one, we couldn't stop shaking. Phyllis decided she'd better get going because she needed to tell Milt the rest of the story. She said, "Milt knows I had a baby girl and placed her for adoption. I told him the story shortly after we started dating. And Delores is going to be so happy to hear that I finally found the courage to tell you the story." Delores was Phyllis's main support from start to finish, and Phyllis would give her this news in person.

We were getting nearer to the finish line. Soon we would know if we could apply for a court order to open the records. I would know soon enough if Phyllis was my biological mother, although I had a pretty good feeling that she was.

"To adopt a child is a great work of love. When it is done, much is given, but much is also received. It is a true exchange of gifts."
—Pope John Paul II

23

September 12, 1990

I went home, walked in the door, and called out, "Bruce, where are you?"

He replied, "Upstairs!"

I ran up the stairs. Bruce had just gotten home from work and had changed out of his work clothes. I said, "I need to talk to you!"

He immediately thought he was in some kind of trouble. "What about?"

"I think I told you that I'm adopted, right?" He nodded. "I think I just met my birth mother today!" Bruce looked very serious and sat down on the edge of the bed. "It's Phyllis Brookbank, Debra's mother. She told me today that she gave birth to a baby girl on May 31, 1955, and placed her for adoption. She thinks I'm that baby girl."

"Really! Do you think you are?" he asked.

"I think so, all of the information matches up, but we're going to get the adoption records opened. She called over to the clerk's office at the courthouse and talked to the judge about it. He asked for all the information about the adoption and said to talk to our families about it tonight and call him back tomorrow morning."

"Wow, that's exciting. Debra would be my sister-in-law!"

"Yeah, crazy, huh! Now I need to call Mom. I'm not sure what to say to her." I was very nervous about that and was sure wishing Dad would be there with her so they could lean on each other. I knew I was going to need to sit down during this conversation, so I grabbed a chair and set it by the upstairs phone hanging on the wall. Shaking, I called her number. After the usual greetings, I said, "Mom, I need to talk to you about something. A couple of years ago, I had this conversation with a customer at Kmart." I went on to tell her the whole conversation, Doug asking me when I started working at Kmart and telling me how I looked like Susan Brookbank. "He was one of Susan's teachers. And I've had that same conversation with a few other people since then. I never mentioned them before because I didn't think anything of it at the time. I even heard the same thing in Minot a time or two, that I looked like somebody."

"Oh really, I didn't know that," said Mom.

"Yeah, I never mentioned that either, because I always had it in my head that I would probably be from one of the Dutch settlements in South Dakota. And besides, the adoption was a closed one, so there was no possibility of opening those records. I found that out when I was nineteen, when Brad and I went on that road trip to the Black Hills."

"Yes, I remember that," replied Mom.

"I didn't give any thought to it after that. At least until now. Anyway, Susan Brookbank's parents attend the Nazarene church. Her mother's name is Phyllis Brookbank. Phyllis is a Sunday School teacher, and she stops by every week to pick up materials for her class. Every time somebody asked me if I was Susan Brookbank, I would tell Phyllis about it at church the next Sunday. Evidently, she's heard the same thing herself."

"Okay," replied Mom. I could tell that she was putting the pieces together.

"Usually Phyllis just says hi as she comes in and as she leaves, but today she brought a coffee pot back and then came into my office and sat down in the chair in front of my desk. She was writing a check for her subscription to our missionary magazine, and I told her that I heard yet another person tell me that I looked like Susan Brookbank. She stopped writing and was looking at me strange. She proceeded to tell me a story from her past. Mom, I think you should sit down for this, if you aren't already."

"I'm sitting down," said Mom, apprehensive. She sounded nervous and a little worried. She knew I was struggling to tell her something and braced herself for it.

"She told me that she gave birth to a baby girl on May 31, 1955, at St. Joseph's Hospital, and she thinks that I might be that baby girl."

I regret not hopping in the car and driving over to tell my mother this news in person. I could have, as she lived only an hour away. I don't know why I didn't. I knew she would be shocked. I myself was still feeling that sucker punch. After some thought, Mom said, "That doesn't necessarily mean anything; it could just be a coincidence. But I think you should get the adoption papers opened so you know for sure. Your dad and I always told you that we'd help in any way we could."

Was she nervous that I would abandon her?

"Yes, we talked about opening the adoption records. She called the judge at the clerk's office and asked what we needed to do to open them. He told us to talk with our families about it first, and if all were agreeable to unsealing the records, then to call him back tomorrow morning and we would talk about getting a court order, which is required. But he especially wanted to make sure that you were on board with it."

"Do you know anything about her or her family?"

"Only that she works at Woolworth's. I used to buy caramel apples from her when I worked at the bank. They had a table out in front of the store during Corn Palace Week every year selling the caramel apples. She has a daughter, Debra, who is friends with Brad. They went to school together, and she is a year older than him. She also works at the truck stop with Bruce. That's about all I know right now, other than that Phyllis has a daughter named Susan, who I've never met."

"And people think you look like her Susan?" asked Mom.

"Yeah, Mom, I think she might be my biological mother. You met her at our wedding—do you remember? She was with Delores Brookbank."

"Oh, I met so many people that day, I can't place her right now, but if I saw a picture of her, I would probably remember her."

"The next time I see you I will bring a picture of her."

"Well, I knew this day could come. If you think she is the

one, you will need to get the adoption records opened to be sure."

"Yes, we definitely will do that."

"You already know that I'm behind you one hundred percent," replied Mom.

"Thank you, Mom. You know that means a lot to me. After we call the judge back tomorrow morning, I will let you know what is happening every step of the way."

"I want you to know that I support you in this, and I always have. Dad and I always stressed that we would help in any way we could when it came time to search for your birth family. I love you very much," said Mom, her voice quivering.

"I love you too, Mom, and rest assured that no one will ever take your place or Dad's. You will always be my Mom and Dad. I will be buried right next to you in the Pukwana Cemetery for all eternity, so you're gonna be stuck with me!" I think she felt a little better about it, but I was pretty sure she didn't get much sleep that night.

I didn't either for that matter. Nor did Phyllis.

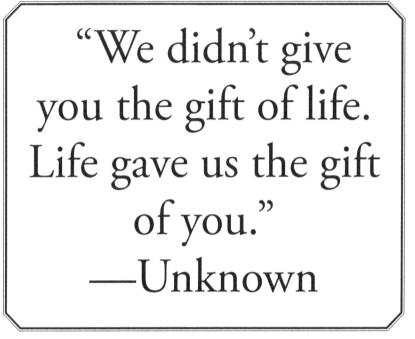

"We didn't give you the gift of life. Life gave us the gift of you."
—Unknown

24

September 13, 1990

On this day, Thursday, September 13, my dad would have been seventy-two years old. I was thinking of Dad that morning and wishing he was with Mom. I knew this was going to be a hard day for her. I wished they could have heard this news together. I went to work at the church after a sleepless night, knowing this was going to be another milestone day. The judge would tell us what the next step was going to be to open the adoption records. I could barely concentrate on my church work.

At about ten o'clock, Phyllis came in, after also having experienced a sleepless night. She was excited and very nervous. She still couldn't believe that she had actually found the courage to say something to me about it. It seemed like a century to her since this all started with Doug Ellwein's comments about her having a daughter working at Kmart.

She was very sure that I was her daughter, and after the previous day, I was pretty sure of it too. Still, we both wanted the court order to open the records. It seemed to take forever for the clock to tick down the minutes to eleven o'clock. Again, the church was so quiet you could hear a pin drop, and the phone stopped ringing.

"Did you notice how quiet it is again?" I asked.

"Yes, this is so weird. I feel like God is making this happen."

"I agree." After all, what better place is there for this scene to take place in than our church? It gave me peace, knowing this was God's will.

"Were you able to discuss this with your mother and family yesterday? Are they all right with opening the adoption records?" asked Phyllis. This was an experience that was intensely personal to us, and it felt strange to talk about our loved ones' reactions.

"It was a shock for Mom, but she's supportive of us, and she offered to help in any way she can. Did you talk with your family?" I asked. I was nervous, anxious, and excited all rolled into one.

Milt knew most of the story already. He knew Phyllis had a baby girl out of wedlock and placed her for adoption. He also heard our conversations at the church about people thinking I was their daughter Susan. What he didn't know was that my birthday was the same day as the baby Phyllis placed for adoption.

"I told Milt the rest of the story last night, and he's behind us 100 percent. We'll know very soon what we need to do for the court order. Are you ready for this?" asked Phyllis. I nodded.

Phyllis picked up the phone, took a deep breath, and, shaking a bit, punched in the phone number. She looked very serious, but inside, she was excited and nervous. "Clerk of courts office. How may I help you?" asked the clerk.

"This is Phyllis Brookbank calling for Judge Gerken. He's expecting my call."

"One moment," said the voice on the other end. Phyllis could hear the beeps from being placed on hold.

"Hello, Phyllis!" answered Judge Gerken. "How are you two doing today after that unforgettable conversation we had yesterday?"

"Well, I can tell you that neither of us got much sleep last night."

"Ha! That's understandable. Did you both have a chance to talk it over with your families yesterday? I especially want to know if you both talked with your husbands and if Sue talked it over with her mother."

"Yes, both of our families are supportive of us, and they are agreeable to the opening of the adoption records."

"I actually have the adoption papers opened and in front of me right now."

"She's your daughter."

"A birth mother puts the needs of her child above the needs of her heart."
—Skye Hardwick

25

September 13, 1990

Neither of us knew what he said after that or remembered hanging up.

After sitting in silence for a minute or two, Phyllis had some things she wanted me to know. She told me my biological father's name and gave me a couple of pictures of him while we were still in my office. I was surprised to see the resemblance to Brad. She said, "He and I never married, and I wanted you to have both a mother and a father. After you were born, the nurse asked if I wanted to hold you, and I said no, the reason being that if I had done that, I never would have gone through with the adoption. I would have kept you, and you deserved more."

I replied, "Yes, my parents were told by their attorney that you weren't married and you wanted me to have two parents. I have much respect and admiration for you for doing that. It was a selfless thing to do. I never once resented you for placing me for adoption."

I knew as far back as I could remember that she wasn't married and that she wanted me to have a father, which she couldn't provide. I believed that she truly wanted more for me than what she could give. I never ever held any resentment toward her. On the contrary, I thought she was wonderful, caring, and selfless.

I asked, "May I ask how you came to the conclusion that I was your daughter?"

She replied, "Well, you and I were talking on the phone one day about church business and we got to talking about you looking like my Susan. And you said that it was really weird, because you were adopted. Well, that got me to thinking. So, I found your birth date, May 31, in the May newsletter. Then, when it was closer to your birthday, I called to wish you a happy birthday and asked how old you were going to be. After you told me, I counted back to 1955. I put it all together then and came to the conclusion that you were the baby girl that I placed for adoption. But I wasn't positive, and I thought I'd better be absolutely positive about it before mentioning it to you."

I replied, "Oh yeah, now I remember telling you that I was adopted. It surprised me that I said that at all, because that's something I didn't talk about."

"I have an idea—let's go introduce ourselves to Judge Gerken," said Phyllis. So, she and I got in her car and drove to the courthouse to see the judge. He had already left for lunch, so instead, we stopped at Milt's Service. Milt was a sweet man, about five feet, seven inches tall with a slender build and a very nice personality and disposition. He still resembled Elvis a bit and was very handsome. He had a nice smile, and I suspect that he made lots of friends with that smile of his.

Phyllis wanted to properly introduce me to him. She said "This is Sue Vrooman, my biological daughter who I gave up for adoption in 1955. The judge confirmed it this morning."

I didn't know how Milt would react to this news. I was a little nervous and anxious, maybe even dreading it a bit. I just didn't know what he would think of me. The only times I'd seen him were at church, so I didn't really know him that well. But what I did know of him, I liked. I was anticipating him shaking my hand, saying, "It's nice to meet you."

Instead, Milt walked up to me, gave me the biggest bear hug, and said, "Welcome to the family!" He didn't have to hug me, and he certainly didn't have to welcome me to the family, but he did. That's Milt. He's had a special place in my heart ever since.

"Thank you, Milt," I said tearfully.

Since I grew up an only child, I had been thrilled when Phyllis told me that I had two half-brothers and three half-sisters. But I didn't know how to act with siblings. They were all so close, how would they react to the news of a new sister? Would they like me? Would they want to have a relationship with me? Did they look like me? What should I say to them? Do I have nieces or nephews? My nervousness matched my joy at finding my birth family.

Phyllis took me back up to the church so I could drive home and call my mom. Mom answered on the first ring as she was awaiting the news. "Hi, Mom. Did you get any sleep last night?"

"Well," she paused, "not really. Have you spoken with the judge yet?"

"Yes, we did. It looks like we don't have to get a court order. Phyllis gave all of the information to the judge yesterday, and he retrieved the papers himself. He had them spread out on his desk. He asked if we spoke with our families and if everyone was on board with opening the records. We told him yes. He told Phyllis, 'She's your daughter.' It was short and sweet."

"Huh, so she really is your biological mother. I never in my wildest dreams would have thought you would find her this way. Goodness! I wasn't expecting that so soon! Will you be able to get copies of those records?" asked Mom.

"We stopped at the courthouse to talk with the judge, but he was out, so we'll try him again next week. We'll have to make some plans for you and Phyllis to meet."

"That sounds good, but not too soon. It's going to take some time for me to get used to this. I *am* interested in meeting her, just not right now. I would like to see the adoption papers though."

"I know, Mom, so would I. I wish Dad was with you. I'll come over this coming Saturday and we can just have a nice day together, okay? We can talk more about it then."

"I like that idea," replied Mom.

"I just want to remind you that you will always be my mom and I will always call you Mom. I will call Phyllis by her name. No one is going to take your place. Okay?"

"Okay. I love you."

"I love you too, Mom. See you Saturday!" I hung up the

phone and decided I'd better get back to the church because I had taken an extra-long lunch break and still had work to do.

Phyllis couldn't believe that she finally had the courage to tell me the story. She had held that in for a year and a half. She was relieved. But the next few days would be a whirlwind of visits and phone calls to and from family members. She was pretty wiped out and decided to go home and rest for a while to get some peace and quiet. The next few days would be crazy.

But before going home, she needed to go see Delores and tell her what she had done. Delores was going to wig out. "Delores!" Phyllis exclaimed, grinning from ear to ear. "You're going to be so proud of me, but you're not going to believe this!"

"What is it?" asked Delores, matching Phyllis's excitement.

"I finally did it! I told Sue my story!"

"You're kidding! Seriously?" replied Delores.

"Yes, seriously! I did it! I finally got the courage to tell Sue that I had a baby on May 31, 1955, and that I wanted her to have both a mother and a father, which I couldn't provide. I told her that I stipulated that she be raised in the Catholic faith and that I made the decision to place her for adoption. I said, 'I think you are that baby girl.'"

"What did she say to that?" asked Delores.

"She said, 'I hope it's true'—can you believe it? I just went to the church to return the coffee pot that I borrowed, and I stopped in to Sue's office to renew the missionary magazine. She told me again that somebody had told her she looked like my Susan. And I swear to you, I heard God's voice speak to me. He said, 'Phyllis, now is the time.'"

"Oh, Phyllis, that's wonderful," said Delores. "I have goosebumps on my arms!"

"That all happened yesterday in her office. We called the clerk's office at the courthouse and talked to the judge about opening the adoption records. We thought he was going to tell us what the next step would be for obtaining a court order. But instead, he just blurted out, 'She's your daughter!' He had the papers in front of him on his desk."

Delores, in tears, gave Phyllis a big hug and said, "Congratulations! I am so happy for you!"

"I wanted to tell you yesterday but decided to wait until we knew for sure today. You were the next person to tell after Milt."

"You know, Phyllis, this was God's plan. He made it happen," said Delores.

"I completely agree, it's definitely not a coincidence," replied Phyllis. "I just realized, too, that I told you on the day of Sue's wedding that this had to be the year I tell her. I just made it." Phyllis left then and went home to rest.

The next person I would give this news to was going to be Brad. He was with me when I tried at the age of nineteen to get a court order to open my adoption records in Mitchell. Brad was only two years old then, so he didn't understand what was going on. We had discussed the subject of adoption a few times throughout his life though, so he was on this ride right along with me.

I took off a little early from work so I could spring the news on him that he was about to meet another grandmother. After all of the conversations I had with people who thought I was Susan Brookbank, I didn't say anything about it to Brad or anyone else, as I didn't think anything of it. I would have to start from the beginning, telling this story to Brad.

When I got home, I noticed his car in the driveway, so I knew he was home. I went upstairs and knocked on his door. He opened the door, and I said, "I have some news to tell you. Can I come in?"

He replied, "Sure! Is this good news or bad news?"

"Oh, it's very good news." I started by telling him about the conversation that happened at Kmart two years earlier with Doug Ellwein. I told him others had said the same thing to me throughout that time. "Every time someone told me that I looked like Susan Brookbank, I would repeat those conversations to Phyllis at church the next Sunday. I didn't give a second thought to any of it."

I continued with the story. "I didn't suspect a thing. Phyllis Brookbank came in yesterday to return a coffee pot, and she stopped in my office to visit for a while. I told her that I heard from yet another person that I looked like her daughter Susan. She sat back in her chair and looked at me funny. She told me then that she had given birth to a baby girl on May 31, 1955, at St. Joseph's Hospital in Mitchell. She said she thought I was that baby girl." I paused. "Well, the judge confirmed it this morning. Phyllis is my biological mother. You have another grandmother!"

"Really? Phyllis Brookbank is your biological mother? Really?"

I nodded, smiling. He was excited and grinning from ear to ear. He kept saying "Really?" over and over.

"Phyllis is my grandmother? This means that Debra is really my aunt! This is crazy! I'm going over to their house." And that's what he did. When he got to Phyllis's house, he said to her, "Did I hear this right? That you're my grandmother?"

"Yes, you heard right!" said Phyllis. She told Brad her story, starting with Doug Ellwein and continuing up to the present.

"You gave me so many more relatives!" said Brad.

Phyllis replied, "Yes, I've given you lots of relatives. Four uncles, four aunts, and four cousins, two here in Mitchell and two in Virginia."

Brad was still recovering from *his* big surprise and completely forgot he had homework to do. Not that he was in any shape to do homework anyway. I was still just as surprised as I was the day before when Phyllis dropped that bombshell of a story on me. And what a story it turned out to be.

Phyllis needed to give this news to her other five kids next. The oldest, Mike, already knew there was a sister out there somewhere, because years earlier, his mother-in-law informed him that there was. Mike wanted to hire a private detective to find me, but Phyllis had told him to leave it be. She didn't want to stir up the past or upset their families. Mike didn't know it at the time, but he was *so close*—he went right by our house every day on his way to work.

Phyllis was determined that Mike would be the first one to meet his new sister. Phyllis called his wife, Kathy, and told her the news, but asked Kathy not to say anything to Mike because it was a surprise for him. It was set up for the next day,

Friday, for Mike and Kathy to come over to Phyllis's house to meet with me and Bruce after we got done with work.

But first, she would call Susan, who was living in Virginia at the time. Susan already knew there was a sister somewhere but hadn't given it any thought in years. She was shocked when Phyllis informed her that she'd found her sister on accident and that her name was Susan also. Susan said to her mother, "But why does her name have to be Susan!"

Phyllis replied, "I didn't name her that; her parents did. They were given a blank birth certificate, and they gave her a new name."

Mary and Scott lived in Virginia also, but neither was home, so Phyllis asked Susan to relay the news to them. Susan said to Mary, "We have another sister, and her name is Susan too. I'm not the oldest sister anymore." Susan was annoyed at this, and kind of sad too. Mary was shocked but happy. Scott was the coolheaded one, and his reaction was, "Another sister? Come on, you gotta be kidding!" Phyllis would tell them the whole story on their next phone call.

Debra, the youngest, was friends with Brad. Phyllis was dreading having to tell Debra, as she didn't know anything about another sister. Phyllis said, "Debra, I need to talk to you about something. A long time ago, I was engaged to be married to a man other than your dad. And I was pregnant. We broke up halfway through the pregnancy. I gave birth to a baby girl on May 31, 1955, and immediately placed her for adoption. We have found each other on accident. Neither of us were looking; it just happened. The baby girl I gave up is Sue Vrooman, Brad's mom."

Debra was surprised, shocked, and annoyed the most of anyone to hear this news. She didn't know anything about another sister. Debra said, "My English teacher, Mr. Ellwein, kept asking me if I had a sister working at Kmart. I kept telling him no. I don't know how many times he asked that, but it was a lot."

"Oh yeah, Mr. Ellwein asked me the same thing," replied Phyllis. "I know this is a shock to you. You've known Brad for a few years now, and you were related to him all along. You're his aunt!" Debra didn't want to hear that, so she marched off to her room. She needed some time.

Phyllis didn't want to forget to tell her sister Dorothy this wonderful news. Dorothy was Phyllis's biggest advocate throughout her life and a big help with her pregnancy. It was Dorothy who taught Phyllis how to change diapers, just in case Phyllis and Ed decided to get married after all, and it was Dorothy who loaned her maternity clothes to Phyllis. It was also Dorothy who helped Phyllis come to the final decision to place her baby for adoption.

She said, "Dorothy, I have a story to tell you, and you're not going to believe it. My firstborn baby girl, Kathryn Lynn Cunningham, has come back into my life." She told Dorothy the story.

Dorothy was in tears. "Oh, Phyllis, God had His hand in this. You were meant to find each other."

"Yes, Delores said the same thing. This is a God-given story for sure." They had a nice long talk that day, and Phyllis told Dorothy all about meeting me at church and of her and Delores being in cahoots when they came to our wedding.

210

I still needed to tell Bruce, Justin, and Jeremy the news. So, when they got home from work, I sprang the news on them that Phyllis Brookbank was my biological mother and that Debra was my sister. Justin and Jeremy said in unison, "Debra's our aunt!" They couldn't wait until they saw her again at work.

That was Thursday. What a day.

The next day, Friday, September 14, I would meet Milt and Phyllis's oldest son, Mike. Phyllis asked Bruce and me to come over after work to meet Mike and his wife, Kathy. Bruce and I got there first, and shortly thereafter, Mike and Kathy came in. We were seated on the couch in the living room. Mike looked over at us, and he looked puzzled, probably thinking, *Who are these people? What's going on here?*

Phyllis came right out and said, "Mike, I want you to meet your older sister, Sue."

His eyes got big as saucers. I stood up, thinking he was going to shake my hand and very politely say, "Happy to meet you," but instead, he bypassed my hand and gave me a big bear hug, just as his dad had the day prior. When he pulled away, he gave me a long look and then hugged me again. We had a good visit that day, and he asked Bruce and me, "Where do you live?"

I answered, "We live at the corner of Minnesota and Third Street. It's a big house built out of crushed granite and has a huge porch on the front."

"No way! I go by your house every day on my way to work."

"If you have the heart for adoption, don't let fear stand in the way."
—Doug Chapman

26

After the Discovery

The Nazarene church finally got its new pastor. He arrived after our story came to light, but he asked us to
give our testimonies at the evening service on Sunday, December 2, 1990.

Mom and Phyllis finally got to meet that afternoon. Bruce
drove to Chamberlain and brought Mom to Mitchell. Mom
and Phyllis had a couple of phone conversations before meeting, discussing the events leading to my adoption. This would
be their first time meeting in person, unless they counted the
time they met at my wedding. They were both nervous, but it
helped that they visited on the phone. We got to the church
early and went in and sat down in the sanctuary. It was quiet
and nobody would come in for a while, so we could visit in
private there.

Mom said, "Hello, Phyllis, it's nice to finally meet you in
person."

"Oh, Marion," Phyllis replied, hugging her, "I have prayed

for you and Sue all these years. I'm so happy that she was adopted into such a wonderful family. I couldn't have picked a better one."

"Thank you, Phyllis, we prayed for you, too, while you were pregnant, although we didn't know your name then. You gave us a great gift. I wish you could have met Jack, her dad." Mom and Phyllis hit it off very well. Both were nervous, of course, but they seemed to get along great.

The pastor introduced Phyllis and me before we gave our testimonies at church that evening. He gave a sermon about a son who had left his family but was welcomed back with open arms. He continued on to say that Phyllis placed her baby girl for adoption, and now they were back together and had welcomed each other into their lives. We told our story to a packed church, as many were quite anxious to hear the whole story.

Phyllis ended her testimony with, "I didn't realize this story would happen because of a coffee pot! If I hadn't brought that coffee pot back, I don't think we'd be up here tonight telling this. I think that coffee pot should be blessed, I really do! We're all so happy. I'm glad it's out. To sum this all up, I just want to say that I've always believed in miracles. I created one, and I have experienced it!"

I told my story and added at the end, "Everyone's been so supportive. Milt and their kids have accepted me into their family. God works miracles, and I believe this is one of them!"

The pastor announced, "What a wonderful reunion. Isn't this great? What better illustration to hear God's message than right here in our own church. God is at work. And all because of a coffee pot! We have a lot of brothers and sisters when we are adopted into God's family. So many have been expressing this feeling of joy and rejoicing. And to think they are both here in the First Church of the Nazarene in Mitchell, South Dakota!"

"Families don't have to match. You don't have to look like someone else to love them."
—Leigh Anne Tuohy

27

After the Discovery

After Judge Gerken opened the adoption records and after the church testimonies, life went back to normal, sort of.

Doug Ellwein was perhaps the most surprised to hear this story, even though he was the one who started the whole thing. He'd been so sure that the Susan who worked at Kmart was Phyllis's Susan; of course, he was right, but not in the way he expected. He was just as shocked as the rest of us to find that I was *another* Susan, and we were grateful that he didn't let it go, because without him, probably none of this would have happened. He was persistent.

Phyllis and I spent the next few months looking at each other's pictures and asking lots of questions. One day at her house, she asked, "Did you live in Huron right from the start?"

I replied, "No, we lived on a farm north of Pukwana."

"Oh, really? For some reason, I had it in my head that you went to Huron right away."

"No, not right away, but we did move there in 1963, and we lived there until 1970, when we moved to Minot, North Dakota."

We had been talking about her relatives who were buried at the cemetery north of town, so we got in her car and headed there so she could show me their graves.

Her parents' graves were first. "Oh, I wish you could have known my mother. She came to the hospital the day after you were born and asked me if she could hold you. I told her yes, but in a different room. I didn't want to see you for fear that I would keep you. You deserved more. So, my mom did get to hold you, and she didn't come back to my room for about three hours. She spent a lot of time with you. I can about imagine that she was giving you the Cunningham family history."

"She sounds like a neat lady. I wish I could have known her," I replied.

"She passed away in 1978, and my dad passed in 1959. I have one brother, Gifford, and my sister, Dorothy, left. I had two other brothers, Clarence and Harvey, but they are both gone. Clarence is buried out here, so we'll go over to his grave next. Harvey is in Sioux Falls." We started walking over to Clarence's grave.

As we were walking, I said, "My dad passed away on Christmas Day in 1983 of cancer. He died at the VA hospital in Minneapolis."

"He was in the service?" asked Phyllis.

"Yes, he was in the Army and served during World War II

in North Africa and Italy. He was overseas for three and a half years."

"We're a military family too—two of my brothers served stateside during World War II, and Mike has been with the National Guard for many years. Milt also served in the Army during the Korean War." We arrived at Clarence's grave.

"Clarence was the sheriff in Mitchell for many years. He was nineteen years older than me, so I was only two years old when he got married. I knew him mainly through his daughter Delores." We started back to the car.

I told her about the great family I was adopted into. I told her that her wish was granted that I be raised in a Catholic family, and boy, was it ever Catholic. We have five monsignors, as well as several priests and nuns, on my mom's Brady side of the family. One of them was Monsignor John Brady of Holy Family Church in Mitchell.

"Did you say Monsignor John Brady? He baptized me!" exclaimed Phyllis.

"Really! Were you raised in the Catholic Church?" I asked.

"No, I was Presbyterian. But your birth father and I were engaged to be married at Holy Family, and to do that, I had to change over to the Catholic religion. One of those things that was necessary was the Sacrament of Baptism. I completed the instructions and was welcomed into the church. I became a Catholic. I'm very surprised to hear that Monsignor Brady was a part of your family!"

She told me about her Cunningham family and how she had traced them back to the 1600s, when her seventh-great-grandfather, William, sailed on the ship *Speedwell* in 1635 to the

New World. Several generations of Cunninghams lived in Virginia, and the eighth generation, Phyllis's dad, Thomas, heeded the call of the West and headed for South Dakota.

"Before I formed you in the womb I knew you,
Before you were born I set you apart;
I appointed you as a prophet to the nations."
—Jeremiah 1:5

28

After the Discovery

Phyllis and I found we had all sorts of things in common. We both have hazel eyes and very fair skin. We are good at math, and while I grew up an only child, she was kind of like an only child since there were ten years between her and her next older brother. Being "only" children, we learned to entertain ourselves, and we had fun doing it. I had a Chinese checkers game that I used to play by myself with five other people, who were all me. And both of us knew several ways of playing solitaire. Being pregnant and unwed was another similarity.

Phyllis said, "My mom found this home for unwed mothers in Sioux Falls that I could live in until your birth, but I didn't want to leave Mitchell, so I opted not to go there."

"Really? I *did* attend one of those in Minot. I was sixteen years old and pregnant, and I had to drop out of school. My mom found the Oppen Home for Unwed Mothers, so I attended classes there during the day and went to night school with my dad to get my diploma."

The best thing we shared was our love of all things Wizard of Oz. When the Mitchell Playhouse put on the production of *The Wizard of Oz* at the old State Theater on Main Street, we each knew one of the performers and went to watch together.

> We're off to see the Wizard, the Wonderful Wizard of Oz!
>
> We hear he is a whiz of a wiz if ever a wiz there was
>
> If ever, oh ever a wiz there was, the Wizard of Oz is one because
>
> Because because because because because
>
> Because of the wonderful things he does
>
> We're off to see the Wizard, the wonderful Wizard of Oz!

Phyllis and I discovered something strange with our names. For starters, there are two Susans. My middle name is Jane, and Mary's middle name is Jayne, with a y. My confirmation name is Theresa, and Mike's daughter is Theresa; also Kathy's middle name is Theresa, and a cousin is named Teresa (no h). Brad's middle name is John. Mike's son is John. My birth name was Kathryn Lynn. Mike's wife is Kathy, and Debra's middle name is Lynn. Both Susans had a dog named Queenie. No coincidences here. It was just further confirmation that God was working on this story of ours.

The attorney my parents hired to handle my adoption told them that I was of Dutch descent. All my life, I thought that my biological family's name probably started with *Van*, *Van de*, or *Van der*. Imagine my surprise when Phyllis told me I'm actually part English, Scottish, and mostly Irish, with a little bit of German and Norwegian, but definitely no Dutch.

Mom was dismayed to find that I was mostly Irish. "You're part Irish? Huh! After all that teasing you and Dad did on Saint Patrick's Day?" My husband makes up for my lack of Dutch as his family *is* from the Netherlands, and some of his cousins' last names start with *Van de*.

Phyllis and I both worked in the sporting goods departments of our respective employers—Phyllis with Herter's and me with Kmart. We both sold licenses and guns. We both worked in the toy departments—Woolworth's for Phyllis and Kmart for me. That was Phyllis's favorite department and mine too. Kmart is where our story began, with Doug Ellwein asking me if I was Susan Brookbank.

Phyllis worked at Woolworth's until it closed in 1993, and I continually bought caramel apples from her every year during Corn Palace Week, even after I left the bank. After our story came to light, I told her that I was the one who picked up caramel apples for the bank back in the early eighties, and her reply was, "Really? That was you? Really?" I was so sad to see Woolworth's close but happy that the Woolworth's caramel apples were still available during that week. Phyllis will always be the Caramel Apple Lady in my book. Woolworth's continued on as Foot Locker.

The new pastor's wife had always done the office work at their previous churches, so she took over our church office duties, and I got my job back at Kmart working in the sporting goods and toy departments. The store had moved to the other side of the highway into a new and bigger building.

Debra worked at the I-90 Truck Haven Restaurant, and Bruce was one of her bosses. When Justin and Jeremy found out that Debra was my sister, they started calling her Aunt Debra. This news was a huge shock for her, finding out she had another sister, and she wasn't having this "Aunt Debra" stuff. Everything she knew changed in the blink of an eye. Justin and Jeremy stopped calling her Aunt Debra, and by the following summer, she was a little more used to the fact that she had another sister named Sue.

Brad graduated from high school in May of 1991. Phyllis and Debra came over for his graduation open house, and he was glad to see them. It was another opportunity for Mom and Phyllis to get together, plus Bruce's mom was there too. Brad got a kick out of having another grandmother.

That summer, Milt and Phyllis hosted a barbecue at their house in honor of all the siblings and grandchildren finally getting together. I was looking forward to meeting Susan and really curious what she looked like. Mary and daughter Megi, Susan and son Mohammed and daughter Sameera, and Scott returned home for a vacation. I was nervous as I didn't know if they really wanted to meet me at all. Would they even like me? Would they talk to me at all? I decided to greet them with a smile and hope for the best. Phyllis stuck to her guns that I looked more like Scott than anybody. Susan and I both agreed we look nothing alike. We were all pretty nervous. It was still a shock to them, meeting another sister they knew nothing about. Everyone laughed when they found out that Justin and Jeremy already knew Debra since they were at the truck stop often after school.

Phyllis and my mom were getting acquainted also with phone calls. Phyllis drove over to Chamberlain a couple of times and took Mom out for lunch at Al's Oasis. There was no shortage of things to talk about. Mostly it was about me though!

Bruce and I continued to spend our date nights at the truck stop restaurant to enjoy those delicious apple pies with ice cream.

"Love is unselfishly choosing for another's highest good."
—C. S. Lewis

29

After the Discovery

Bruce and I continued on at the Nazarene church until 2001, when we moved to Superior, Wisconsin. Superior is a city in Douglas County in northwestern Wisconsin. Situated at the western end of Lake Superior, Superior is connected to Duluth, Minnesota, by a bridge over the harbor and forms the metropolitan area of the Twin Ports. They share a harbor, a very important port on the Great Lakes. Their main exports are grain, coal, iron ore, limestone, and turbine components. The lakers (Great Lakes ore carriers) and salties (oceangoing vessels) load and unload their cargoes beginning in March at the docks. The Twin Ports have ship entries at Duluth and at Superior and are the farthest inland freshwater seaports on the Great Lakes. Lake Superior is the largest freshwater lake; all the other Great Lakes can fit into Lake Superior with room left over. The Duluth entry is used the most, and tourists can see the ships up close entering or leaving. The Superior entry was the final port of call for the ship *Edmund Fitzgerald* before it sank with all twenty-nine men aboard in 1975.

It was hard for us to move and leave our families, but they knew that it was a great opportunity for Bruce to work for the Frito-Lay company. I transferred after nine years from my Kmart in Mitchell to the Kmart in Superior, at which I would work for another twelve and a half years. We promised to keep in touch with everyone through visits and phone calls.

Phyllis loved the obituaries section. It didn't matter what town or what state the deceased person was from. She loved to read about their lives and to see who survived the deceased. She especially loved the ones who lived long lives. She rejoiced with them and hoped she would live a long life also. After we moved to Wisconsin, I sent her the *Superior Telegram* obituaries a few times. Phyllis would call and say, "I just *love* reading those obituaries! I didn't know any of these people, but I wish I did because they're so *interesting*!" Emphasis on interesting.

Living in Superior, I discovered that we lived only an hour and a half away from Grand Rapids, Minnesota, the home of Judy Garland. The Judy Garland Museum is there, and the house she grew up in is attached on the backside of the museum. As a little girl, she was a part of a singing trio called the Gumm Sisters. The museum also houses the original buggy used in the movie with Abraham Lincoln's signature on it (he used it while campaigning for president), and one of four pairs of ruby slippers. In 2005, the museum was broken into, and the ruby slippers were stolen. Several years later, they were recovered at the bottom of a lake, ruined.

Every year in June, Grand Rapids would host the Judy Garland Festival, and the living Munchkins were honored guests. I attended the festival every year and met Meinhardt Raabe (the coroner), Jerry Maren (the Lollipop Kid), Margaret Pellegrini (a villager), and Karl Slover (a soldier). I got autographed pictures from all of them, and Meinhardt Raabe and Jerry Maren both autographed pictures for Phyllis, which she got for Christmas.

> As coroner, I must aver,
>
> I've thoroughly examined her.
>
> And she's not only merely dead,
>
> She's really most sincerely dead!

Since the discovery, there were weddings, funerals, and many births. Debra added five more children, and then the grandchildren started having families of their own. Phyllis's grandchildren were often the topic of our phone conversations. She was very proud of her grandchildren and great-grandchildren. Phyllis was the matriarch of a rapidly growing family, and it's still growing.

Her sister, Dorothy, passed away in 1993; her brother Gifford passed away in 1999; and her husband, Milt, passed away in 2000. Phyllis could often be heard saying, "My parents are gone, my brothers, sister, and husband are gone. Why do I have to be the last one left?"

My answer to that is, "Somebody has to be the last one left. Why not you?"

"As soon as I saw you, I knew an adventure was going to happen."
—Winnie the Pooh

30

After the Discovery

In 2004, my mom's doctor called me with some awful news about an aneurysm that was threatening her life. I was in Wisconsin, so I took some time off work and visited Mom.

"I have an aneurysm that is in the blood vessels leading to my heart. Surgery could help, but I don't want to have surgery." She started to cry. "I just can't go through that."

I was worried. I wasn't ready to lose her. I replied, "If you don't want the surgery, I won't make you have it, Mom, but I don't want to lose you." I hated having to go back home to Wisconsin and leaving her.

Dreading what she had to do, and not telling me about it, Mom picked up the phone and called Phyllis. She broke the news to her about the aneurysm and asked Phyllis if she would be willing to step into her place when the time came. Phyllis said, "Yes, absolutely, I consider it an honor that you'd ask me. I absolutely will." That was a difficult phone call for Mom to make, but she must have felt comfortable

enough with Phyllis to do it. Phyllis sat there stunned for a while as she knew that it had to have taken every ounce of courage Mom had to make that call and she had probably been thinking about it for days or even weeks. The love she had for my mom was indescribable. I would find out about that conversation years later. Phyllis said she would get goose-bumps reliving it.

On April 9, 2005, Mom was getting ready to go out for lunch with some friends and was in the bathroom putting on her makeup when it happened. The aneurysm worked its way to her heart. It was sudden. One minute she was on Earth, and in a split second, she was called Home. Her funeral was held in Chamberlain, with burial in the Pukwana Cemetery. She was cremated, and I was holding her urn as we were driving out to the cemetery, talking to her the whole way. There was an old Dairy Queen building that had been abandoned and sat next to the road. I said, "Mom, we're going by the old Dairy Queen, and the windows are still intact!" We would always be amazed at the windows still being intact and not broken all those years, and we always would make a comment about it. "Now we're going up the hill, Mom, on your final journey."

Phyllis met a lot of my relatives that day. She loved Mom and all of my family very much. When Phyllis went home that day after the funeral and lunch afterward, she had a very happy heart. After meeting my cousins, aunts, and uncles, she felt such joy that she placed her baby girl with such a wonderful family. She told me that many times throughout the years.

We took a trip to Germany to visit Jeremy and family at the end of 2007, and we went on a road trip to see the Steckelberg castle ruins. I took lots of pictures and showed them to Phyllis. She said, "You have a castle? I really *did* give you to a good family!"

Phyllis and I talked about writing our story for years. We've told this story to hundreds of people and wanted to write it for a magazine or a book. We agreed that we both needed to sit down and start writing our story. The next time we'd meet, the same conversation would take place, but nothing got done. We told the story for our church newsletter, and we called it "God Still Works Miracles." This is a God-given story, and we give Him the credit. Neither of us knows what His reason is for bringing us together at this time. Phyllis said, "I'm glad it happened now and not earlier."

Phyllis moved out of her house in 2010 and into an apartment. She wasn't too sure about apartment living and didn't bring too many things with her from the house. As time went on, she liked living there more and more. One phone call would have her complaining about the place, and the next call would be more positive. She eventually grew to love it there.

She was in her apartment seven years before the time came when she needed to go to the Firesteel Nursing Home in November of 2017. This is when I understood that I was under pressure to get our story written. She liked it at the nursing home and knew several of the residents. She had a very small room, but she had her television and some Wizard of Oz things to keep her company, and of course, the pictures of her wonderful mom and dad that Brad tacked up on her bulletin board. She had her family pictures, along with a stuffed bear that Mary made, on a shelf above her television set. These were her most prized possessions.

"You don't choose your family. They are God's gift to you, as you are to them."
—Desmond Tutu

31

After the Discovery

Since the day that Judge Gerken opened the adoption records, we never got around to getting copies made of them. And now Phyllis was in a nursing home. I thought to myself, *Where did the time go? It's too soon! I still have lots of questions!* I called the clerk's office to get copies, but they said I needed to get a court order. I said, "But the adoption records have already been opened. We just didn't get the copies made at the time."

The clerk replied, "You have to get a court order every time they are opened. I'll send you the paperwork to get started."

Since a lot of the conversations with Phyllis included a desire to see those adoption papers, I got busy starting the process to open the adoption records again; it would be a long one. Many forms had to be filled out: the application itself, a letter explaining why I wanted to open the records, and an information sheet with the name the records were under. This time I knew the name was Kathryn Lynn Cunningham. It was a slow process and took a few months, but I eventually received all of the records, plus two birth certificates—the original one in the name of Kathryn Lynn Cunningham, and the other in the name of Susan Jane Steckelberg. Unfortunately, my parents never got to see the first one.

I surprised Phyllis with them in March of 2018. Mike joined us, and I said to her, "Phyllis, you know how we never got around to getting copies of the adoption records and we kept saying we should get them?" She nodded. "Well, I have a surprise for you!" I handed her the stack of papers. "Do these look familiar to you?" She looked them over and saw the word *adoption,* and her eyes got big and wide.

She exclaimed, "Really? You got the adoption papers? Really?" She read every word. She kept saying, "I can't believe this! Do you know how many years it's been since I've seen these papers?"

Laughing, I answered, "Yes, I do!"

While looking at the birth certificate, Phyllis noticed that

it said "unknown" under "father." "I wonder why I did that?" she questioned. While I was doing research on birth mothers surrendering their babies in the 1950s, I found that all of them had "unknown" in the spot where the father's name went.

When she finished reading them, she went on to proudly introduce me to every person in the nursing home, saying, "This is Sue, my biological daughter whom I gave up for adoption on May 31, 1955." It felt good to be introduced to her friends, and to know that she approved of me enough to show me off. Everyone I met offered their congratulations and said that we looked alike. We were both pretty proud of each other.

Although we had the adoption papers, we had yet to write our story. I realized that I'd procrastinated way too long. I decided to make a few trips to Mitchell and interview Phyllis. Brad came with me on one of those trips, and he recorded Phyllis talking about her life. I got a lot of information that day. She talked about her mom and dad and how they spoiled her. She talked about Ed and his mother a bit. She talked about her children and grandchildren, and how she now has several great-grandchildren besides. She also talked about her mother finding the home for unwed mothers in Sioux Falls. Brad and I listened very closely. I was taking notes as she was talking.

Other visits were ones where her hearing aid wasn't working very well, so I wrote out the questions. She answered verbally, and I wrote down her answers. I have pages and pages of notes. I could tell that her memory would sometimes betray her as she would be talking about Susan doing this or that, but it was really her own mother she was talking about. Overall, she did pretty well, and I was able to decipher what she meant.

Phyllis and I had lunch and supper together on my trips there. She was assigned a certain table to sit at, and the lunch workers set a place for me too. While waiting for lunch to be served, the ladies at our table introduced themselves to me, so Phyllis told them a shortened version of our adoption story. Soon, people from other tables came over to shake my hand. By the end of that first lunch, I had met most everyone in that lunchroom. When supper came and I walked in, everyone waved hello to me, and one very sweet gentleman yelled out, "Hi, Sue, glad you're joining us again!"

We discussed those May baskets with all the petals that had to be cut out, and she would act disgusted. She'd say, "Honestly, I can't believe nobody would help me cut out those petals! They probably don't even make them anymore because nobody wants to cut out the petals!"

Phyllis passed away peacefully on September 20, 2018, at the age of eighty-six, in her room at the nursing home. She joined her beloved family members who had been saving her a place in Heaven. Five days later, her prayer service was held at Bittner Funeral Home in Mitchell.

Phyllis's funeral was held the next day at her church. The kids and grandkids milled around in the basement and waited to go upstairs for the start of the service. Mike shouted, "Susie! Where are you? Come up here. You're the oldest—lead us in!"

Well, I'm rarely speechless, but that comment rendered me speechless. It's a good thing I was sitting down. I walked to the front of the line and stood in front of Mike, and when the funeral director said, "It's time," I started up the steps and proudly took the lead of Phyllis's children coming into the sanctuary. I felt honored to do that, and more so, that my half-siblings wanted me to.

She definitely went out in a blaze of glory. She had many wonderful kids, grandkids, and great-grandkids to carry on her legacy. She was buried at the Servicemen's Cemetery next to her husband, Milt. She left some very big shoes to fill.

Ever since that day in my office when the judge confirmed the adoption, I had saved adoption stories from the paper and magazines and copied them to give to Phyllis. I also did that with any stories about the Wizard of Oz. All of these stories were spread out on a table at her funeral.

Phyllis loved angels. She had angels all over her house and on her tree at Christmas. Now she *is* one.

"Family is not defined by our genes. It is built and maintained through love."
—Amalia G.

Conclusion

Note from Sue's son, Brad

Just a few weeks after my mom made her final edits to this book, she was diagnosed with glioblastoma (brain cancer). A skilled team of surgeons removed a majority of the tumor, and she completed radiation treatment and two rounds of chemotherapy. She remained in high spirits throughout her battle with cancer, which lasted over five months, until she passed away peacefully on May 21, 2022. We never know how many days, months, or years lie ahead, and this illness has been a reminder of that fact!

Her husband Bruce and I both know how important this book was for her. It is our privilege to publish her story for you to read. I had the honor of traveling with Mom and recording some of her interviews with Phyllis and other relatives. Before Phyllis passed away, Mom promised that she would write down their story. By God's grace, she was able not only to fulfill that promise, but also to see and touch a copy of this book in her last days before passing on to her Heavenly home.

I hope you've enjoyed learning about our families and the amazing ways that God showed up through this story. The following paragraphs are Mom's concluding thoughts and family updates. Enjoy!

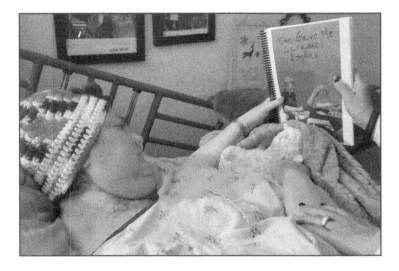

And here we are, scattered around the country again. Susan moved to Morgantown, West Virginia, to be by her son and daughter. She is working two jobs. Mike stayed in Mitchell and still lives in the old home with Kathy. Mike retired in 2019 after forty years with the South Dakota National Guard and is now selling electronic components on eBay, plus working on Milt's old service station, which Mike now owns. He's also tearing the main floor of the house apart and moving walls around, making it a completely different house. He's already added a basement to it. Mary lives in Rapid City, South Dakota, with her husband, Terry. They are blessed to have all of their children and grandchildren close by. She has been working with her credit card company for thirty-plus years. Scott moved to Orlando, Florida, and is working at Universal Studios. Debra lives in Mansfield, Texas (a suburb of Dallas), and is raising her two youngest, a boy and a girl. She works for an optometrist. She returns to South Dakota often as her family is growing rapidly. I live in Superior, Wisconsin, with my husband Bruce, and am retired. I'm the oldest and am now on Medicare. I have a few more wrinkles, and my crow's feet have their own crow's feet.

What a journey this has been. I was perfectly content waiting until death to find out who my birth family was. I already had a great family, and I was happy. And then September 12, 1990, happened. For Phyllis to deliver that story to me when she herself was scared to death was an awesome thing. I know that this was God's will. I don't know why yet, but I'm hoping that He will reveal the reason to me someday.

I have a great family in the Steckelbergs, Moores, and Bradys, and the Cunningham and Brookbank families have accepted me also. This story has changed me in a way that I'm more interested in hearing others' stories about their adoptions, and I'd like to work as an advocate for adoption, either for people looking to adopt, or for the adopted child looking for his or her biological parents. I try to encourage those who are looking for their birth families. I'm very lucky, but not everyone is as lucky as I was. Some stories are such that maybe one party isn't interested in meeting their relative or that once they do meet, they want nothing to do with each other. Sadly, I've heard a few of those stories. I feel for them.

Phyllis and I shared a love of genealogy. I have seven notebooks dedicated to the Steckelberg, Moore, Brady, and Cunningham families, four of them Steckelbergs alone. I feel like I'm a part of all of them. Even though I "found" my birth family, I still feel the family connection with the Steckelbergs,

Moores, and Bradys. The Cunningham and Brookbank families are icing on the cake.

I have family members all over the United States and the world and would love to visit them someday and to make a return trip to Germany to fully explore the Steckelberg castle ruins and grounds.

I will always remember Phyllis talking about those pesky May baskets and her disgust at being the only one to cut out the petals. And I will never throw out the LTD catalog anymore, since Phyllis believed that the sun rose and set for those catalogs. Every Christmas season, that poor catalog of hers went through heck and back. She always found things she couldn't live without or that any of us couldn't live without.

While Mike, Susan, and Debra were mentioned in this story several times, Mary and Scott were not because they lived in Virginia, and we didn't get very many chances to be together. Susan is mentioned a lot, of course, but we haven't been together much either. I had the opportunity in 2019 to spend a few days with Mary, and we had a wonderful time. We are planning on more of those visits. Hopefully, there will be some opportunities available like that with Susan and Scott.

Now I'm starting my new venture as an author, following in the footsteps of John Brookbank, with his book *Cancer? But I'm a Virgo!* available on Amazon and at Barnes and Noble. Nice promoting job, huh, John!

Brad gave Bruce and me DNA kits one year for Christmas and we sent them in. My DNA confirmed that Ed is, indeed, my birth father.

Photo Gallery

Sue with all five Brookbank siblings in September, 2018 (L–R: Sue Vrooman, Mike, Susan, Mary, Scott, and Deb)

Sue with her husband, Bruce, at the White House (Washington, DC, 2018)

Sue with her son Brad at the NorShore Theater's production of *The Wizard of Oz* (Duluth, MN, December 2019)

Sue at the entrance of St. Anthony's Catholic Church (Pukwana, SD, September 2021)

Epilogue

I have come to realize that things do happen for a reason. Looking back on my life, I've come to see that God was guiding me the entire way down this path. The events, both good and bad, were God's will. I didn't know it then, but I know it now.

One of the bad events is the night I went out with my girlfriends after my breakup with Jim. The night I met David, we could have gone to a different place, we could have gone an hour earlier or later, or even on a different night. Why? I didn't know it then, but God meant for me to meet David that night. I really wanted to leave out the part where David and I married. That is a part of my life that I would like to put in the back of my brain and forget. I hated having to bring back those bad memories. It was uncomfortable to write, but I had to include that in order for the story to unfold. After all, David is the reason I ended up back in Mitchell.

From breaking up with Jim, to meeting David, to leaving the Catholic church and attending the Nazarene church, my life was orchestrated by God. It was the same with Phyllis. It was His plan to get Phyllis and me together somehow.

Phyllis had quite a life. She had been through the Great Depression, the World War II years, Ed, his mother, and a pregnancy. She went through a lot during that time. She had many things to consider as far as her baby was concerned, and she opted for adoption. It took her a while to get back to normal. Then she met Milt, she had five more children, and the rest is history. Phyllis is gone now and is in Heaven, along with her husband, parents, and siblings.

God directed me and Phyllis every step of the way through our lives. I know without a doubt that this story is God given. I know that the good things and the bad things that happened were of God's design. He puts those situations in front of us so we can get over the hurdles and continue on. This is how we grow in God. I feel stronger now, knowing that these hurdles are put in front of me for a reason. I know that God has my life in His hands. He calls the shots. I am content that He knows what He wants from me. God had His hand over Phyllis and me throughout our lives, guiding us.

In the Introduction, I stated that a normal person would find many coincidences in our story. I don't believe in coincidences. Maybe one, two, or even three are okay. In our case, there were so many of them that I believe nothing in our story is a coincidence.

People come and go in our lives. Some stay, and some just pass through. The moral to this story is that life is a cycle. We experience both pain and happiness. Our sanity depends on it. We just have to trust that things will turn out okay. There is no need to worry about our future. God already knows our future.

I still don't know the reason why our story happened, but there is one. Phyllis knows the reason now. I'm patient. I'll know soon, if not in life, then in death. I'll wait.

Acknowledgments

Mom and Dad, when it comes to parents, I couldn't have chosen any better. I was one very lucky girl, and I always knew that you chose me to be your daughter. Everything I am today is from your teaching and guidance. You taught me respect, honesty, responsibility, and generosity. You brought me up in the Catholic faith. I am a Christian, and I dedicate my life to God. I thank Him for you, Dad—you taught me how to fish (I loved our fishing trips) and drive (we practiced parallel parking in the high school parking lot). Mom, you are my anchor, my friend, and my advisor. You prayed with me and dried my tears. You always and forever will be my mom. You taught me how to budget, and you both listened to me practice my violin. I'm sure there was a time or three you wanted to join the dog in the basement with all that screeching. I probably gave both of you every one of those gray hairs, especially in my teen years. I give you two the credit for making me the balanced person I am today. I've had a full and happy life, and I have you to thank for it. Thank you for choosing me, Mom and Dad. I love you. Until we meet again.

Phyllis, it took a lot of strength and courage for you to choose adoption. It's the most selfless act there is for a mother. I'm very grateful to you for the hard decisions you had to make, and I have so much admiration and respect for you for that. God had His hand over us, guiding us through life, getting us to this place. Any little change that would have been made would have altered our story. I thank God for you. He is the reason why we can tell this story now.

"My birth mother brought me into this world, but it was my adoptive parents who gave me life."
—Christina Romo

Thank You

To: Phyllis Brookbank, for telling me her story and answering questions in writing when her hearing wasn't very good.

To: Delores and Ivan Brookbank, for filling in a lot of the blanks.

To: Mike, Susan, Mary, Scott, Debra, and Nona Moore, for answering hundreds of questions.

To: Mary, for going through pictures with me and allowing me to borrow a bunch.

To: Brad, for keeping me on track and introducing me to Positive Adoption Language, and for filling me in on some things long forgotten.

To: Doug Ellwein, for relaying your story about your persistence that I was Susan Brookbank. Without you, this story probably would not have happened.

To: Toni Brill, John Brookbank, and especially Victoria at Wise Ink Creative Publishing, for the editing.

To: Father Andrew from the Superior Cathedral for the information on Catholic adoptions and on becoming a Catholic.

Some Adoption Information

Part 1: Definition of Adoption

Adoption means legally becoming the parent of a child born to someone else. The parent assumes legal responsibility for the child, and the child has the same rights as a child born to a biological parent. When you adopt, you become more than the legal parent—you become that child's mom or dad. Whether a natural child or adopted child, they are different only in the process, not in the result.

Who is the true parent then? Is it the one who bears the child or the one who raises him or her? Birth and adoptive parents want the same thing for their children—to grow up happy, healthy, safe, and loved. The answer is that the true parents are the ones who give that opportunity to their children. So, birthparents *and* adoptive parents achieve this goal together.

Part 2: The Steps to Adopt

1. Make the decision to adopt. These reasons can vary from not being able to bear children, to not *wanting* to bear children, or anything in between.

2. Decide on a domestic or international adoption. This entails adopting in the United States or outside the United States.

3. Find an adoption agency or adoption attorney. The major difference between the two is the cost and the wait.

4. Fill out the application. After this step, things get moving.

5. Home study. The courts use this study to determine if a stable environment exists in the home. To make an accurate assessment, the courts literally want your life history.

6. Home visit. Upon successful completion of these steps, the application to adopt is reviewed and considered for approval.

Part 3: Closed, Open, and Semi-Open Adoptions

Closed Adoption, a.k.a. Confidential or Secret Adoption: In a closed adoption, an infant is adopted into a family and the biological parent's record is sealed. The biological father's name is usually not recorded, even on the birth certificate.

**This was my case exactly.

Open Adoption: In an open adoption, the adoptive and birth families have contact and share personal information like names, addresses, and phone numbers. They can have regular meetings. The contact can be before and after the adoption with phone calls and visits. Many adoption agencies do *only* open adoptions.

Semi-Open Adoption: A semi-open adoption is similar to an open adoption, in that the adoptive and birth families can have contact, but no personal information is exchanged. The birth mother chooses the adoptive family after reading many applications. She may decide she wants to meet them. After the adoption, letters and photos can be exchanged through the agency or attorney.

Part 4: Agency Adoptions

Agency adoptions fall into two categories: state agencies and private agencies. The downside to choosing a private agency is finances. Adoptions through the state are generally less expensive. Most private agencies base their fees on income. The fee is less when adopting older children. Private agencies usually place newborns. The wait can be up to two years for either state or private agencies.

Part 5: Attorney Adoptions

Another way to adopt is through an adoption attorney. There are some attorneys who can do the same things as an adoption agency. They will work with the adoptive family to locate an available child. Most work with infant adoptions. Working with an attorney is more expensive, but you will receive a placement faster, usually within a few months. The fees can be several thousand dollars. Plus, you may also need to pay the birth mother's medical and living expenses.

Part 6: Finding an Agency or Attorney

Ask for adoption literature and a meeting from each option. Pick one that is licensed, that has several years' experience, and whose license is current.

Part 7: The People Involved

There are many people involved in your adoption quest:

1   The birth mother—whether you have contact with her or not, she'll be important because she is the one who made it possible for you to adopt her baby.

2   The social worker—she is your advocate, and she keeps you informed on the adoption process.

3   The attorney—the attorney will file the adoption petition and all other necessary documents pertaining to the adoption. If you're working with *only* an attorney, he or she also takes on the role of adoption agency.

4   The judge—the judge makes everything final and will be your favorite person in the world.

Don't think the adoption is over then; it's just started, and it lasts a lifetime!

Part 8: The Waiting Period

This is a good time to get the nursery ready, paint a room, and attend classes at the hospital on caring for newborns. And sleep—because soon you won't get to sleep very much.

Part 9: The Placement Period

This is a busy time as there are baby showers, never-ending company, and sleep deprivation. However, the adoption isn't finalized just yet. It will be finalized after the placement period, usually two weeks to three months. The social worker will make two or three visits to see how you're doing with the child. If all is well, she will submit her report to finalize the adoption.

Part 10: Finalization of Adoption

The attorney will file a Petition to Adopt in court. The final hearing happens after the placement period is over. The adoptive parents, attorney, and someone from the agency will attend. The judge signs the papers, and the parents and the child are declared a family.

Part 11: Tell the Story

After the judge declares your child adopted, tell your child his or her adoption story immediately; that way, your child will grow up knowing it right from the start. There will be no surprises later.

**My parents read me the book The Chosen Baby *by Valentina P. Wasson for as long as I can remember. Other books that are wonderful to read are* I Wished for You: An Adoption Story *by Marianne Richmond and* Let's Talk About It: Adoption *by Fred Rogers.*

Some adopted children will have the feeling that they were abandoned. Focus on the fact that your child was wanted and loved. Your child was chosen.

> ****I never felt abandoned. I always knew that my birth mother wasn't married and couldn't provide a father. She couldn't raise me alone. I've always understood that.**

Adoption is for a lifetime. It's a big part of a child's life, but it's not the deciding factor for his or her life. It *will* be important sometime throughout his or her life, however.

I used *Adoption for Dummies* as a guide for this information.

I have much praise for the television show *Long Lost Family* on the TLC network. This program showcases a birth mother or birth parents searching for her or their child, or an adopted child searching for his or her parents. I highly recommend watching these programs. All of the shows that have aired have been positive, with happy endings for both parties.

Recommended Books

For Adopted Children:

The Chosen Baby by Valentina P. Wasson
I Wished for You: An Adoption Story by Marianne Richmond
I've Loved You Since Forever by Hoda Kotb
Let's Talk About It: Adoption by Fred Rogers

For a Birth Mother:

Those Three Words by Christine Bauer
I'll Always Carry You: A Mother's Story of Adoption, Loss, Grief, and Healing by Linda L. Franklin
The Book of Answers from Your Birth Mother: A Guided Journal for Birth Mothers to Share Their Life Story by Jenny Lynn Delaney
The Girls Who Went Away by Ann Fessler (Highly recommended!)

For the Adoptive Family:

Chicken Soup for the Soul—the Joy of Adoption by Amy Newmark and LeAnn Thieman

Chicken Soup for the Adopted Soul by Jack Canfield, Mark Victor Hansen, and LeAnn Thieman

Honestly Adoption by Mike and Kristin Berry

Twenty Things Adopted Kids Wish Their Adoptive Parents Knew by Sherrie Eldridge

Finding the Birth Family:

All You Can Ever Know by Nicole Chung

Young Love: An Adoptee's Memoir by Bonnie Parsons

Swabbed and Found: An Adopted Man's DNA Journey to Discover His Family Tree by Frank Billingsley

A moment in
my arms, forever
in my heart.

Made in the USA
Monee, IL
10 September 2022